DAYDREAM
BELIEVER

DAYDREAM BELIEVER

UNLOCKING
THE ULTIMATE POWER
of YOUR MIND

MITCH HOROWITZ

author of *The Miracle Club*

Published 2022 by Gildan Media LLC
aka G&D Media
www.GandDmedia.com

First Edition: 2022

Front cover design by Tom McKeveny
Front cover photo by Ebru Yildiz
Back cover photo by Jacqueline Castel

Interior design by Meghan Day Healey of Story Horse, LLC.

Library of Congress Cataloging-in-Publication Data is available upon request

ISBN: 978-1-7225-0577-6

10   9   8   7   6   5   4   3   2   1

To Neville

"My metaphysics are to the end of use.
I wish to know the laws of this wonderful power,
that I may domesticate it."

—RALPH WALDO EMERSON,
Powers and Laws of Thought

Contents

Introduction

The Will to Create

"What are all beliefs but the possibilities of I?"
—AUSTIN OSMAN SPARE, *THE FOCUS OF LIFE*

Several years prior to this writing, a famous political operative—someone you would immediately recognize and perhaps be surprised by—asked me to meet him at a suite in a posh Park Avenue hotel. I biked up from my then-home on Manhattan's Lower East Side. As I settled into a sofa with my helmet in my lap, he asked me: "Who is the best writer in New Thought?" My questioner referred to the philosophy of positive-mind metaphysics that began in the transcendentalist ferment of New England in the mid-to-late 1800s and mushroomed across the nation.

"Neville," I immediately replied, referring to Neville Goddard, one of the most intriguing mystical voices of the past century.

"No," he said, ribbing me—"I didn't ask who's the coolest, I asked who's the best."

I repeated my assessment. The British-Barbadian Neville, whose career spanned from the late 1930s until his death in California in 1972, was a resplendent speaker who, under his solitary first name, wrote more than ten books on the limitless powers of thought. He has been my greatest influence. But I have differences with Neville's ideas, which I do not believe cover the full gamut of human crises and mortality. I wondered then as I have other times: who could I recommend unreservedly?

Although I do not approve of the actions of the political figure who put the question to me, I nonetheless determined to allow it to serve as a personal goad. I decided right there to adopt it as my challenge to lay out a metaphysics of thought causation that shied from neither the sublime heights of possibility nor the severity of the barriers facing us. Ralph Waldo Emerson wrote in his journals of February 22, 1824: "If Knowledge be power, it is also Pain."

Daydream Believer is the result of that effort. It deals with the interdimensional and infinite nature of your psyche—by which I mean a compact of thought and emotion—and also the paradoxical limits that create the tension of existence.

This book considers your psyche's causative abilities, practically and theoretically; it responds to the ablest critics of mind-power metaphysics; it presents the evidence for extra-physical mentality, which is overwhelming; and it considers the role of ethics in thought causation. I equate ethics with reciprocity. And reciprocity, as I use it, is a wild force not to be understood as simple cause-and-effect between individuals but as part of a vast cycle of action and reaction within the human symmetry. Reciprocity must be approached with great care and acknowledgment of one's limited perspective.

My hope is that *Daydream Believer* takes the last 150 years of experimentation in New Thought to its sharpest peak and sets us on a path for the next stage. More importantly, I wish that the book shines a light for your own practice and experiments, frames mind-power as a meaningful response to life, and provides you with the tools to surpass its insights. If you find my claims bold, I trust that you will find my self-disclosures—necessary for any honest reckoning of practical philosophy—equally so.

*   *   *

What is the purpose of a spirituality of personal creation? "All events that result from intention are reducible to the intention to increase power." Friedrich Nietzsche wrote those words in 1885–1886 in his notes to an incomplete and posthumously published book *The Will to Power*, as translated in 1967 by Walter Kaufmann and R.J. Hollingdale. Let me be plain: that is my driving principle in this book.

When people speak of pursuing truth, peace, understanding, freedom, justice, forgiveness, patience, or faith, they are indirectly identifying means to power: to the growth of their capacities for expression, attainment, and connection to the source of causation and creation. To argue against this framing inadvertently demonstrates its activity. Philosophies seek primacy.

"Desire is a manifestation of power," wrote Wallace D. Wattles in *The Science of Getting Rich* in 1910. A leading light in New Thought, the socialist and metaphysical explorer belonged to an early and influential strain of positive-mind philosophers.

Indeed, I believe that a great deal of what gets defined or expressed as neurosis is the frustration of the power-seeking impulse in the individual—not power as brutality or force but as *self-agency*. If that impulse can be validated and reawakened, rather than explained away, then anxiety, fear, or hostility can often be transformed. I write this from personal experience. But I must add two serious notes of caution. First, experience also compels me to note that certain baseline traits of behavior seem likely to follow a person to some greater or lesser degree for a lifetime. There may be a complexity of reasons for this (or, possibly, one simple reason that exceeds our focus here: reincarnation); whatever the case, we seem to never wholly shed a particular emotional thumbprint. My second caution is to watch for the tendency toward overcompensation for past disempowerment. I have also witnessed this in myself. Exercising personal power and self-determination can serve to right past wrongs and foster personal happiness; but it can also, at times, result in a too-ready capacity to act rashly or sever ties. It can lead to selfishness. I have hurt others in this way. It was never my wish to do so. But medicine is in the dosage.

*   *   *

Because it addresses the practical needs of life—money, intimacy, health, self-image—New Thought, or the spirituality of mind causation, has proven enduringly popular since it took modern form in the late nineteenth century. But New Thought culture has proven more adept at popularizing than at refining its ideas. With the death of philosopher William James in 1910 (the year before Wattles and the same year as Christian Science founder Mary Baker Eddy and transcendentalist medium Andrew Jackson Davis), few serious efforts have emerged from within New Thought's sprawling, informal culture, of which I count myself a part, to confront and resolve the philosophy's inadequate response to suffering, both physically and emotionally, both intimately and on a macro scale.

"The cabalists, like the Gnostics," wrote historian Richard Cavendish in his 1967 history of the occult *The Black Arts*, "set out to answer questions which confront any religious thinker. If God is good, how has evil entered the world which God created? If God is merciful, why is there pain and suffering in life? If God is limitless, infinite and eternal, what is the connection between God and a world which is finite, limited in space and time?"

In recent decades, New Thought has done too little to probe these questions; many of its practitioners rush to ascribe every event to thoughts, either individually or in the "race consciousness;" and current New Thought philosophy does almost nothing to meaningfully confront the discordance between wish and event in the experience of the seeker, other than to say: *try again*. Trying again usually involves some variant of *assuming the feeling state* of your wish fulfilled. Although I honor that familiar approach, and believe in its utility, I am not single-minded on the matter. It is simply impractical and psychologically unfair to impel a suffering, grieving, or frightened person to "change" his or her feeling state to foster a desired outcome.

Indeed, recent to this writing, I heard from a suicidal young man who had previously experienced success with the methods of Neville Goddard to whom this book is dedicated. As alluded, Neville has been a vital influence on me. His contention is that *your imagination is the creative force symbolically called God in Scripture*—and that everything you experience is yourself out-pictured into the world. Neville's key method is to emotionally "live from the end" (a phrase tattooed above his visage on my upper left arm) or view yourself from the *feeling state* of the wish fulfilled. I do not accept this approach as absolute. Alternate methods, along with supports that may be nonspiritual in nature, are urgently needed. The young man I mentioned had some early breakthroughs but then encountered intrusive thoughts, perceived failure, and desperation. I replied to him in part:

> Hello, I am sorry to hear of that and I think I understand some of what you are going through. Neville is wonderful—but we must also accept that our emotions run on their own track and they cannot always be controlled, nor should they. Also, I believe that what happens to us in life can trace a long arc. Suffering today can be the basis of something much greater tomorrow. Life is a polarity.

I also encouraged him to seek medical and therapeutic help. Mind metaphysics is not an exclusive path.* Insofar as we avail ourselves of it, mind-power philosophy must acknowledge friction and suffering; its acolytes must prove capable of confronting life without leaning on homiletic quotes or catechistic references handed down generation after generation, or in translation upon translation, of canonized spiritual literature. We need a spirituality of personal verification and results.

We must also shed the shibboleth that "positive thinking" produces the same kind of personality: rosy, ebullient, upbeat. Positivity takes many forms, including deliberateness, persistence (what some call faith), and dedication to evaluating events based not on whether they produce happiness, which may be fleeting, but on their potential for fostering personal development and self-expression.

*   *   *

Nothing that I have written is cause to reject New Thought and its affiliated expressions, which often go under what I consider the inadequate (and, in this book, revised) terms "Law of Attraction," "Power of Positive Thinking," or "manifesting." Rather, what I describe is reason to reform New Thought.

We need a revitalized New Thought: one that remains spiritual, which is to say extra-physical. In its history, New Thought has been largely right about the limits of philosophical materialism, or the belief that matter creates

---

* See my appendix, "Depression and Metaphysics."

itself. New Thought's pioneers evinced a powerful instinct for current findings in placebo studies, neuroplasticity, autosuggestion, mind-body medicine, as well as insights in psychical research, string theory, and interpretations of quantum mechanics.

What future advances might a revitalized New Thought and its practitioners foresee? For this potential to be realized, we require a New Thought in which intellectual excellence is seen not as a barrier to feeling but as a conspicuous embarrassment in its absence. In short, a New Thought that warrants its name. By the end of this book, that is what we will have, together. And I vow to you: we will get there through sharing the truth of the search, not as idealized but as lived.

Chapter One

The Power of a Single Wish

"And with the wish the energy was born . . ."
—*CORPUS HERMETICUM*, BOOK I

I am going to use this chapter to challenge a piece of New Thought orthodoxy. As noted, by New Thought I mean mind causation or what is popularly—and, in my view, unsatisfyingly—called manifestation or Law of Attraction.* In attempting this challenge, I hope to pro-

---

* The term "law of attraction" began in the work of medium Andrew Jackson Davis, who in 1855 produced a six-volume treatise on metaphysical laws, *The Great Harmonia*. In volume four, Davis defined the Law of Attraction not as a principle of cause-and-effect thinking but as a cosmic law governing the cycles and maintenance of life. "The atoms in human souls," Davis wrote, "are attracted together from the living elements of soil and atmosphere; and, when these atoms complete the organization or individuality, they then manifest the same law of Attraction in every personal relation, inward and outward, through all the countless avenues of existence!" In Davis's rendering, the Law of Attraction was a mystical force of affinities ever-present in cosmic and human affairs. Among other things, the law dictated where a person's soul would dwell in the afterlife based on correspondences he or she had displayed on earth. The popular remaking of Davis's law as a force of material gain began in 1892 in journalist Prentice Mulford's pamphlet series, *Your Forces, And How to Use Them*.

vide an option that may prove distinctly powerful for you. But you can make that determination only through personal effort.

Let me begin where many experiments in ethical and spiritual philosophy do: with a memory. It is a memory that I cannot quite verify in its accuracy. Nor can I prove it empirically in its details (which I have tried to track down and failed). But I recall it as vividly as though it occurred yesterday. Other people were in the room when it happened and if they were to read this passage, I expect that my recollection would basically square with their own.

Many years ago, during my publishing career I was an editor at a political imprint, which was foundering and seeking new directions. I am often leery of media outlets seeking new directions, since I think problems are solved by doing better at fundamentals rather than pursuing novelty. In any case, at a weekly editorial meeting, an editor—I do not recall who—mentioned that an accomplished literary journalist wanted to write a nonfiction book on the power of a wish. The publisher at the time perked up and said that he thought it sounded like a good idea. I agreed. The book, to my knowledge, never got written. But its theme haunted me.

The unrecalled journalist was, to my understanding, approaching this study of wishes from a non-spiritual perspective. But what, after all, is spiritual or non-spiritual? I believe that our lives include an extra-physical aspect, evidence of which shows up, for example, in statistically based academic studies of ESP, precognition, and retro-causality (when a future event impacts the past, such as better recall now of something you will memorize later*). I return to these and related ideas, and evidence for them, throughout this book. Moreover, Einstein's theories of time and relativity and ensuing experiments have demonstrated that time is a mental device not an objective reality. Time slows based on speed or gravity. Hence, an event that someone encounters in the so-called future may be something another person experiences right now. Given the conditional basis of reality, I believe, and consider it unavoidably necessary to conclude, that our perceptions play some part, impacted by other laws and forces, in selecting those events we experience.

Within this nonlinear reality there exist infinite possibilities—not prospectively, I aver, but actually. Nearly a century of experiments in quantum mechanics demonstrate that a subatomic particle exists in a state of potentiality in which it is infinitely dispersed—until someone takes a measurement at which point the object assumes locality. This observation is augmented by the so-called many worlds theory of quantum physics in which alternate outcomes—including past, present, and future—are determined by the actualizing effect of measurement.** Measurement is the decisive factor on

---

* E.g., see "Feeling the future: A meta-analysis of 90 experiments on the anomalous anticipation of random future events" by Daryl Bem, Patrizio E. Tressoldi, Thomas Rabeyron, Michael Duggan; *F1000 Research*, 2016, updated 23 July 2020. I consider this study in detail in chapter twelve, "The Parapsychology Revolution."

** The only certainties about quantum physics are the data it records and the applications it permits. All explanations of "what's happening"—however matter-of-fact sounding—are conceptual: they are interpretations, models, and theories, often affirming the preferences of the interpreter, a caution that I must also take into account.

the subatomic scale. And what are our senses and perceptions but organic tools of measurement? Now, finely
tuned micro-measurements in controlled conditions *do
not* necessarily reflect the nature of our aboveground,
macro lives, in which we function under a vast complexity of forces. Mental-emotive perspective, even if
framed as law, is not the sole factor at work. For one
thing, laws bend based on circumstance. Water is gas,
liquid, or solid depending on temperature. Yet it must be
granted as a reasonable proposition, based on a century
of discovery, including in new fields like neuroplasticity
where thoughts are proven to impact brain biology, that
thought and perception play a role that exceeds cognition
and motor function alone. That is a basic part of what I
consider my spiritual outlook. It is also why I favor the
term *selection* over manifestation.

So, if time is nonlinear, and if all events are available
as potentialities—a subject that I further explore—I can
sympathize with a principle that Japanese essayist and
novelist Yukio Mishima laid down in his personal mani-
festo *Sun and Steel*: "Anything that comes into our minds
for even the briefest of moments, exists."

*   *   *

The power of a wish returned to me when I wrote the
opening chapter of my 2014 history of the positive-mind
movement, *One Simple Idea*. I called the chapter "To Wish
Upon a Star" and was referencing just that when I wrote
of my adolescence:

In the late 1970s, my family made an ill-fated move from our bungalow-sized home in Queens to a bigger house on Long Island. It was a place we could never quite afford. After moving in, my father lost his job and we took to warming the house with kerosene heaters and wearing secondhand clothing. One night I overheard my mother saying that we might qualify for food stamps. When the financial strains drove my parents to divorce, we were in danger of losing our home. Walking back from a friend's house at night, I used to wish upon stars, just like in the nursery rhyme. Since any disaster seemed possible, any solution seemed plausible.

I *wished upon stars*. A desperate late-childhood indulgence inherited from folklore reprocessed through entertainment—or something more? At a crossroads in my search, I decided to find out. Or at least to determinedly approach the question.

I have often argued that reaching an absolutely clarified idea of what you want in life and to which your life is dedicated—success writer Napoleon Hill called it a Definite Chief Aim—is vital to activating the fullest qualities of your psyche, including the selective capacities for which I argue. For full mental-emotive potential to be reached absolute focus is required. This is true of all measurements. It also mirrors a natural law: focus produces force. Depending on density, currents of air or water can be waved away or navigated—but if channeled into a concentrated stream the same forces may grow irresistible.

Light photons are indetectable to the eye—but if condensed into a laser they can bore through rock. There is no reason to assume that the efforts of the psyche, whether psychological, metaphysical, or both, form an exception. The fields of placebo studies and neuroplasticity alone tell us that expectancy or conviction is *physically measurable.** Not always and not in every case; but enough so that we know this as a circumstantial law. This data is not controversial. Only its implications are.

All of this suggests not only the validity of the New Thought or mind-causation thesis, *but also a different way of working with it.*

As noted in the introduction, a longstanding belief found and argued for in New Thought literature is that the "master key" to mental causation is adopting the *feeling state* that you have received your desire. Hence, countless spiritual writers, including my intellectual hero Neville Goddard, have argued that if you can assume the emotional conviction of your wish fulfilled, often through using a mental scene or picture, you are enacting the selective forces that I have just described. I honor that idea. I have long experimented with it and found it possessed of validity, if unevenly. But I also have a serious problem with that approach. And since I cannot imagine that my life or experiences are exceptional, you may recognize this same problem in your own practice.

When I am in a state of anxiety, such as that surrounding the adolescent events I described earlier, I find

---

* Neuroplasticity, referenced earlier, uses brain scans or MRIs to track the manner in which sustained thoughts alter the neural pathways through which electrical impulses travel in the brain.

it nearly impossible—and sometimes even ethically unde-sirable—to assume the emotive state opposite of what I am experiencing. I cannot always picturize or persuade myself—and, perhaps more importantly, I do not always *want* to persuade myself—of a different feeling state. Happiness is not the only emotion toward which I strive. The passion that arises from the drive to correct a sense of injustice may, for example, convey the same vigor of life that happiness does. The reparative impulse is an impas-sioned force. Its myriad forms are not always to be tamed or contented through amending moods. Hunger com-mands variegated satiety. You would not eat the same meal every day and expect to find it satisfying.

Since I am discontented with, and sometimes even opposing of, adopting a feeling state that may run counter to where emotion finds me, I wondered: Can a wish—even though expressed in future versus present terms—acti-vate the mental selectivity I am describing, and thus heighten the prospect of desired ends?

Now, in New Thought philosophy we often hear that desire, while a positive goad to the seeker, is itself *not* the royal road to victory—and that desire may, in fact, deter victory. A state of desire, it is often said, displaces your need into the future. And there it remains. Hence, a desire, if over-indulged, is a self-perpetuated state of want. You will always feel hungry and never full. This justifies the need to *assume a feeling state of fulfillment*. That is the traditional New Thought reasoning. I find that outlook valid up to a certain point; but in some cases, it is limiting and even restrictive to the individual who is emotionally distraught or physically in pain, which are basic crises of the human situation.

*   *   *

I began to think more broadly about this problem—and a potential way out—after considering a pair of innovative studies that recently emerged from Harvard Medical School's program on placebo research. In 2010, researchers from Harvard's Program in Placebo Studies and the Therapeutic Encounter (PiPS) published a landmark paper, "Placebos without Deception."* Clinicians divided 80 sufferers of Irritable Bowel Syndrome into two study groups: 43 into a no-treatment group and 37 into an "honest placebo" group. Subjects in the latter received a transparently administered placebo. "The placebo pills were truthfully described as inert or inactive pills, like sugar pills, without any medication in it," the researchers wrote. "Additionally, patients were told that 'placebo pills, something like sugar pills, have been shown in rigorous clinical testing to produce significant mind-body self-healing processes.'"

Among subjects in the active group, 59% reported sustained and lasting relief compared with 35% in the control group, which is statistically very significant. Amid a swirl of media coverage, the researchers—to their credit—resisted interpreting or speculating over their results. But the outcome suggested that belief in the facility of the placebo effect was itself sufficient to trigger a therapeutic response. Under the right conditions, the decoy is superfluous.

---

* "Placebos without Deception: A Randomized Controlled Trial in Irritable Bowel Syndrome" by Ted J. Kaptchuk, et al., *PLoS ONE*, December 2010, Volume 5, Issue 12

In 2016, PiPS and collaborating researchers published a second paper on the transparent placebo, this time among 97 sufferers of lower-back pain in Portugal.* Once more, the subjects, 76 of whom completed the trial, were divided into two groups: a no-treatment or control group and a group administered a transparently inert substance with the understanding that a placebo response was being tested for.

"There was," the researchers wrote, "a clinically significant 30% reduction in both usual and maximum pain in the placebo group compared to reductions of 9% and 16% in usual and maximum pain, respectively, in the continued usual treatment group." Moreover, "honest placebo" subjects reported a 29% reduction in "pain-related disability" compared to near-zero in the control group.

We possess clear evidence that therapeutic benefit can be triggered without the benevolent deception generally relied upon in placebo trials. The success of the transparent placebo experiments heightens my interest in whether we can enact the creative agencies of the psyche without attempting to dramatize, picturize, or otherwise imaginatively construct an idealized outcome. I ask us to consider whether belief in mental-emotive agency is *by itself sufficient* to tap greater energies of self.

*   *   *

* "Open-label placebo treatment in chronic low back pain: a randomized controlled trial" by Cláudia Carvalho, et al., *Pain*, December 2016, Volume 157, Number 12

Here is what happened when I challenged the truism of experiencing the *wish fulfilled*—when I instead substituted an *impassioned wish* for a feeling of gratification.

One Monday afternoon recent to this writing, I felt defeated. I was experiencing a sense of career stagnation. My emotions were tormented. The previous week I appeared in a major piece of media, but the project did not receive the support I expected and, for various reasons, I felt dejected. That was not all. I wrote a publisher I admire to gauge his interest in a new project and heard nothing back. After all these years, I wondered, why do I still have to weather this kind of thing? Various other issues were weighing on me.

I took a nap and slipped in and out of consciousness. This "in between" state, as I have often written, is a supple frame of being called hypnagogia. During that period, your body is extremely relaxed and your psyche is open to suggestion. You may, for example, experience dreamlike visions or even hallucinations. During hypnagogia, however, you retain control over cognition. For that reason, hypnagogia is considered "prime time" for mental suggestion. As I explore in chapter twelve, psychical research has also correlated hypnagogia with heightened evidence for anomalous perception and telepathy.

While I laid there, my mind returned to the question of wishes. I was not in the right state to assume an emotive sense of outcome. I was too emotionally tense, frazzled, and vulnerable. I could not adopt a feeling state of victory. But—*I was in a state of deep desire.* Rather than attempt to transmute that desire into something else I instead *framed it into the wish of what I wanted.* What did I wish for? It was at once too broad and too intimate to reveal. But my wish encompassed resolutions to the dilemmas just referenced.

In about a half hour, I arose from my bed and found in my email inbox a satisfying reversal to my disappointment with the media appearance; my hosts were now promoting it. The following morning, I heard from an author I admire who asked for my personal help on a project. I also found a collaborator who could assist me with a major technical problem, which in turn opened a path to a new media opportunity. I reconnected with another publisher I respect and with whom I had long been out of touch. (In the months ahead, that relationship rekindled and resulted in an important contract.) I heard from a podcast producer who extended an offer to me. Most of this occurred within the first two hours of awakening.

Happenstance? Well, very possibly. But not as a prima facie conclusion. We have documented too much in the nature of thought correlating to event, some of which I have already referenced, to embrace any one answer immediately. Or to resort to the overused concept of "confirmation bias," a social-sciences term for prejudice, which afflicts the one who wields the charge as much as the subject toward whom it is directed. It seems to me a worthy personal experiment that a wish, even if expressed as a longing, which is, after all, the nature of any wish, may be a natural, powerful means of mental selectivity. Powerful because it is unforced, focused, and possessed of similar qualities as picturizing. *A wish clarifies.*

And a wish is never "just" a wish. A true wish is not a formula for passivity or a license to idle. If felt authentically, a wish organizes your life with a *sense of duty*. It informs your actions. A wish prioritizes. It may also select.

I write this observation because I recognize that emotions are seismically powerful. Emotions do not always want to be "controlled." Nor can they be. But an impassioned wish—focused, inwardly stated, possibly spoken aloud, and written down (more on which shortly)—employs extant emotions rather than attempts to restructure prevailing ones. For this reason, wishing may feel more natural than picturizing. It may even be more powerful because it meets us as we are rather than where we feel we must be. No one fails at a wish.

*   *   *

Based on what I have described, I ask you to attempt this technique:

1. As you complete this chapter, ask yourself—without embarrassment or self-censorship—what you really, truly want. It can be intimate, material, situational—anything. Be sure your emotions are expressed in earnest. Damn all internalized peer pressure or "spiritual" ideals. Be honest.

2. When forming your wish do not confuse means with ends. You do not necessarily need to focus on one singular solution. Things reach us by many roads. Do not hem yourself in.

3. Hold that wish. Speak it aloud. If you are alone, in nature, or on a platform as a train arrives *shout it*.

4. Write it down. Clearly and plainly. Take the slip of paper or card on which you have written your wish and place it in your pocket. If possible, wrap it in clear packing tape to protect it. Carry it like a talisman. The very act clarifies. It also creates something.

5. Run your wish through your mind as often as possible.

6. Pray for your wish to whatever Greater Force you seek a relationship with. (I explore this theme further in chapter six, "Why Prayer Works.")

7. Recite your wish as you drift to sleep, i.e., in the highly suggestible, mentally subtle state of hypnagogia, and do so again as you awaken.

Record what occurs. Try.

Chapter Two

School of War

The previous chapter on the power of a wish arose due to a need. Its experiment grew out of a state of emotional frustration. Frustration that began on a Friday afternoon, receded and persisted throughout a weekend, and returned with a vengeance on a Monday. I felt a sense of unrewarded effort; incomplete realization; uncertain future. You have probably experienced the feeling of nagging, persistent, and perhaps chronic discontent that I am describing.

It is not to be willed away.

The fact is: life consists of polarities, and of polarities within polarities. Without the call of necessity and the striving toward repair—which also results in frictions—we would remain emotional children. If not for deficit and setback, we would experience no goad toward growth. Ralph Waldo Emerson wrote in his journals of July 28, 1826:

Satisfaction with our lot is not consistent with the intentions of God & with our nature. It is our duty to

> aim at change, at improvement, at perfection. It is our
> duty to be discontented, with the measure we have of
> knowledge & of virtue, to forget the things behind &
> press toward those before.

Although my points of reference differ, I honor that observation. I live by it. The notion of "just being" or realizing
one's current perfection—rather than the *ongoing drive*
toward perfection—is a promise hinged on self-denial. In
my observation, not in literature but in life, it tears the
seeker in two. It often results in passive-aggression, a
malady of New Age culture, to which I return. Can you
imagine anything more self-contradictory than someone
arguing for the position of letting go? I have witnessed this
more times than I can count. I suspect you have, too.

Friction refines. This is what Friedrich Nietzsche
meant when he famously wrote in *Twilight of the Idols* in
1889: "*Out of life's school of war*: What does not destroy me,
makes me stronger." This statement is often quoted—and
perhaps overquoted—as "what does not kill me . . ." but
I prefer Walter Kaufmann's 1954 translation. Whether
overquoted (or overstated), Nietzsche's observation
captures a core truth; his statement cannot be fully
understood in isolation—the philosopher's work must
not be cherrypicked for self-justifying aphorisms, but nor
can his principle be ignored; it stands on its own terms,
as do most of Nietzsche's maxims. Tension, resistance,
and bouts of defeat are the forces that drive intention,
improvement, and resilience.

Now, of course, I desire a "yes" and not a "no" from
life. But if I received only the former, I would experience

no incentive toward the strength, however fitfully realized, to which Nietzsche refers.

Based on what I have written, I was originally planning to title this book *School of War*. But I came to feel that, in addition to it sounding a bit overwrought, that kind of title might overshadow an equally vital idea, also found in *Twilight of the Idols*: "Nothing succeeds in which high spirits play no part." This time I use the 1968 translation of R.J. Hollingdale. I try to note my sources because I discourage the habit of writers who randomly reference unmoored "inspirational" quotes, sometimes in margins, for effect. This kind of practice runs rife in New Thought culture, and it has for too long.

For example, writing in 1897 in his preeminent popularization of New Thought, *In Tune With the Infinite*, Ralph Waldo Trine referenced, and widely popularized, a quote from philosopher and dramatist Johann Wolfgang von Goethe (1749–1832) about the magic of taking action. You probably know it. It has been reprinted thousands of times, including on refrigerator magnets, motivational posters, and in page-a-day calendars. The passage does not lack poignancy—but Goethe did not exactly write or utter it. Irish poet John Anster wrote the lines in 1835 in his very loose translation of Goethe's epic drama *Faust*. The passage appears in a dialogue in the play's prelude:

> Are you in earnest? Seize this very minute:
> What you can do, or dream you can, begin it;
> Boldness has genius, power, and magic in it.
> Only engage and then the mind grows heated;
> Begin and then the work will be completed.

A less romantic but highly regarded translation by Martin Greenberg from 1992 puts the same passage this way:

> It never arrives if you hesitate timidly.
> You say you're a poet, good, very good,
> Let's hear it, then, your poetry.
> You know what's wanted, good strong stuff—
> To work now, work, go right at it.
> What's put off today, tomorrow's put off;
> How precious to us is every minute.
> A resolute spirit, acting timely,
> Seizes occasion by the short hairs,
> It won't let go but hangs on grimly,
> Once committed, it perseveres.*

Both passages possess value and insight. I deem both true. But they intersect only glancingly. Each, in its way, however, supports the gambit of this chapter: challenge ignites action. At the same time, we are involved in the game of life not solely for challenge—but for realization, victory, and attainment. The actuality of success cannot always be satisfied or substituted by the sometimes-doleful learning that emerges from failure or frustration. A New Thought minister I respect once observed, "Understanding is the booby prize." I admire her frankness. (Too rare in such

---

* *Faust: A Tragedy, Parts One and Two, Fully Revised* (Yale University Press, revised 2014). I am also partial to a lesser-known 1949 Penguin Classics translation by Philip Wayne: "The process waits. Then up, begin it!/ What's left to-day, to-morrow's still to do./ Lose not a day, but straight prepare,/ And grasp your chance with resolute trust,/ And take occasion by the hair,/ For, once involved in the affair,/ You'll carry on because you must."

pulpits.) We must be blunt in *naming* what we want; plain about whether we have received it; and brave enough to acknowledge that understanding in itself cannot fill an empty stomach.

In that vein, I offer a passage from Austrian-English poet Erich Fried's (1921–1988) elegy, *Allende Perhaps*:

> I am tired of defeats
> but tireder still
> of friends who come after each defeat
> and prove: 'Actually, it was a victory'
>
> They talk like that
> so as not to be so tired of defeats
> that they succumb to them
> But that kind of talk
> leads to that kind of victory*

What is the proper attitude toward the conundrum that Fried describes? Although a victory lost is a necessary prod to effort, loss alone cannot, as alluded, be equated with or used to substitute for a goal achieved, even when a defeat proves educative. There exists another subset of cases in which what first appears as a loss is later understood as a relief, when the sought-after relationship, task, or commitment might have been deleterious or even disastrous. This is a category to which I will return.

---

* From *100 Poems Without a Country*, translated by Stuart Hood (John Calder Publishers, 1978).

*   *   *

As a guide to outlook and progress when dealing with setback or success, I want to make a new sounding of the oft-heard term positive mental attitude, or PMA. Depending on your temperament, the practice of PMA can be elusive or come naturally. For me, it is the former. I am not by nature optimistic; I am anxious by temperament, something probably reinforced by conditioning, as most personality traits are. Anxiety can be a burden and source of depletion. That is among the reasons I have dedicated myself to the study and practice of positive-mind metaphysics. For me, it is a lifelong effort.

I am aware that something as benign sounding as a Positive Mental Attitude can seem like weak tea in a world filled with stressors, aggravators, social cruelty, and myriad complexities. But let us look again. Although some of the earliest references to PMA appear in Napoleon Hill's *The Master Key to Riches* from 1945, I was turned onto the concept from a different source: the pioneering D.C.-based punk-reggae band Bad Brains. One of the group's guiding lights, lead singer and song writer H.R. or Human Rights, actually discovered Napoleon Hill during his adolescence in Washington, D.C., in the 1970s. It changed everything for the fiercely independent street kid and future punk innovator.

In 2017, H.R. told writer Michael Friedman, Ph.D., in *Psychology Today*:

> I was doing more drugs and living wild. At that time, I knew in my heart that I wanted a better way. Just in the nick of time, God taught me how to relate to

him. It was in 1979. My father introduced me to a book called *Think and Grow Rich*. So, I read the book and found the connection to God . . . it introduced a new philosophy to me. The new philosophy was PMA. Anything the mind can conceive and believe, the mind can achieve.

Artist, activist, and punk chronicler Mark Andersen recalled in *Finding Joseph I,* an oral history of H.R.:

Joseph [H.R.] read the book, and by all accounts, it absolutely altered the direction of his life. *Think and Grow Rich . . .* you think, *Oh, well, it's some sort of goofy get-rich thing.* Well, yeah, but it's also a spiritual book, talking about how people live their lives . . . The idea being that you have to have a reason to be here and without that purpose to focus on, you're gonna be lost. And whether you want a revolution, or you just want to make a good living, it all starts with this can-do attitude. That hit Joseph so hard that he actually started becoming kind of an ambassador for it. He took it around . . . They began to use concepts from Napoleon Hill's book in their music.

More recently a resident of Baltimore, H.R. told John Barry of the *Baltimore City Paper* what PMA and *Think and Grow Rich* meant to him: "It was saying, if you do it in your mind, if you get your mind right, you can do anything. It had this dramatic change in my life. I decided I would use it in my day-to-day living and I would put the lyrics and the message in the songs."

The artist kept his word. He formed a fusion band in 1976 called Mind Power—but soon took matters in a more hardcore direction when the group changed its name to Bad Brains. The inspiration came from the Ramones' song "Bad Brain" and the perception that *bad* is street code for *good*. In early 1982, the quartet Bad Brains released its eponymously titled debut album on cassette: an epic credo mixing punk, hardcore, and reggae. No one else sounded this way. The cassette-only launch is now widely considered one of the landmarks of punk. Its keynote is the guitar-thrashing "Attitude" with the lyrics:

> Don't care what they may say
> We got that attitude!
> Don't care what you may do
> We got that attitude!
>
> Hey, we got that PMA!
> Hey, we got the PMA!

In tribute, I have a lightning bolt with the letters PMA—the band's insignia—tattooed on my left bicep.

Andersen observed that the band itself could even be considered what Hill called a Master Mind group, a mutually supportive alliance of like-valued seekers:

And what they created out of all these pieces is something unprecedented. You can see its roots but it's something entirely new at the same time. I think it was the mastermind alliance Napoleon Hill suggested, the ideas of *Think and Grow Rich*: the PMA, the intense focus, which, to H.R., looked exactly like what he would conceive a band to be. Four individuals pulling together the power of their minds, their hearts and all of their skills towards one objective with intense dedication, focus and concentration. That is what created this incredible entity called Bad Brains.

Hence, when critics in academia or journalism suggest that purveyors of PMA fit into one easy cultural box or category, or they detect superficiality in programs of motivational therapeutics, I tell them: you have no idea.

Yet it must be acknowledged that there *are* times when PMA can feel very distant. Indeed, it is sometimes necessary to express objections, needs, and protests. That is part of life. But our experiment in this chapter is to determine the fullest extent to which our needs can be framed in ways that are affirming of possibility and utility rather than as repetitive complaints, in which we are heavily conditioned to indulge. I grew up in an atmosphere where complaining formed the basis of most conversation and I realized only later in life how encompassing complaining can become and how natural it can feel. PMA healthfully disrupts that.

Positivity sometimes means repose rather than action. There are moments when clear paths forward do not present themselves. In such cases, rather than making one further entreaty to someone or trying one more angle on a problem, we may need to wait and improve our skills, knowing that cyclical changes in social relations and commercial fields are as inevitable as those seen in nature.

But in no case should PMA imply some perfumed or artificial outlook on life. Just as we should never reject talk of victory or attainment so should we never hide from setback or failure. From my perspective, PMA is entirely different from forced optimism. PMA means an *attitude that favors development*. Hence, authentic PMA does not require greeting setbacks with manufactured cheer—although I would not be so quick to discount the mental fortitude of some individuals to whom that is possible—but rather to search through opposition for avenues of refinement and to reenter life with reconstituted plans and projects without falling into the trap, alluded to in Erich Fried's poem, of substituting understanding, perhaps of an ersatz variety, for victory. That would mean accepting the "booby prize."

No—we are in this for victory: for unrestricted and maximal expression of self. But since friction is inevitable, and since it is a requisite to growth and revision, PMA seeks, whenever possible, to *evaluate circumstances according to their potential for self-expansion and refinement*. Within this framing also exist natural or metaphysical laws that come to our aid, a theme explored in chapter six on prayer.

* * *

The extraordinary spiritual philosopher P.D. Ouspensky (1878–1947) made a valuable observation about the nature of a positive attitude in a talk to his students reproduced in the posthumously published book, *A Further Record: Extracts from Meetings 1928–1945*. In its lowest and least useful iteration, Ouspensky said,

... a positive attitude does not really mean a positive attitude, it simply means liking certain things. A really positive attitude is something quite different. Positive attitude can be defined better than positive emotion, because it refers to thinking. But a real positive attitude includes in itself understanding of the thing itself and understanding of the quality of the thing from the point of view, let us say, of evolution and those things that are obstacles. Things that are against, i.e., if they don't help, they are not considered, they simply don't exist, however big they may be externally. And by not seeing them, i.e., if they disappear, one can get rid of their influence. Only, again it is necessary to understand that not seeing wrong things does not mean indifference; it is something quite different from indifference.

What the teacher is saying, albeit on a very great scale, is that the individual must seek to understand forces that develop or erode his or her humanity, itself an immensely large question. Hence, we are not concerned with conventions of good or bad, happy or sad, but with questions of *developmental forces* and what they mean to us.

On that note, I return to Nietzsche: "Whatever is not a condition of our life *harms* it." This is from Kaufmann's 1954 translation of *The Antichrist*, written in 1888 but considered sufficiently controversial so that its publication was delayed until 1895. Implicit in Nietzsche's statement is the imperative found in a true positive attitude: to progressively disassociate yourself from everything and everyone that does not fulfill the needs of your development.

This echoes a contemporaneous statement by William James in his 1899 essay *The Gospel of Relaxation*: "It really looks as if a good start might be made in the direction of changing our American mental habit into something more indifferent and strong." By *indifferent*, the philosopher meant capacity for mental determination and loosening of concern rather than emotional reactivity and obsessiveness—an attitude, what we are calling PMA, that steps past the unnecessary, which is anything that hinders us with secondary emotional concern and unconstructive expense of energy.

A word of caution: never mistake the principle of deliberate selectivity for an offramp from personal debts, deadlines, and commitments. Or as a self-serving excuse to break your word. Whoever cannot keep his word can do nothing. Indeed, none of what we are exploring here is intended to make your life or obligations any *easier*. Rather, it is intended to establish a new metric that loosens the hold of the extraneous and reduces judgments of "good and bad"—which are generally emotional expressions of perceived safety or peril—in favor of a new scale of evaluation that views conditions based on their potential for fostering resiliency, power, and development. That is PMA. Sometimes one must pass through the School of War to experience it.

Chapter Three

The Truth About Mind Causation

A t a professional lunch, an editor and friend once asked me: *"Can we manifest?"* As noted earlier, I disfavor that term. But I also believe in replying to a blunt question with a blunt response. The simple answer I offered my friend is: yes. You should be heartened if you find my supporting argument in this chapter persuasive. But you should also take whatever truth it offers very seriously in its implications and demands. Because no force requires greater maturity of its user than that which is radically simple in power—and overwhelming in effect.

* * *

I value records of individual experience because I firmly believe that no life is exceptional, not mine, not yours, and many of us can relate to things felt, seen, and undergone by another. The clarity of relating such experiences, and the ability to sustain doubt or allow for the prospect of other stories, outcomes, and emphases, are usually the markers of some kind of universally pertinent personal episode, one that applies in general terms to the life of someone else as it does to you. Human universality is one of our great gifts. It makes life navigable.

In that vein, I want to convey to you an intimate experience that I believe intersects with—and speaks truthfully to—your existence. It struck me with the force of existential fact.

As I once walked through the darkened streets of a slightly humid Brooklyn spring evening and reflected on my life up to and encompassing of that moment, I realized with an overwhelming sense of actuality that *life assumes the contours of consistently held thought.* (In fact, what you just read was the first line written of this book.) The arrival of this perspective or realization—which I suspect you have also felt at one time or another—may be experienced as a surprise; it may reflect myriad joyous or painful possibilities; it may convey an understanding of how others have been affected (and raise questions, too, about the ultimate nature of all our experiences, a point I revisit in the next chapter); it may present you with momentary awareness of the impact of your alienated or unacknowledged selections; and it may leave unanswered critical questions—such as the seismically powerful force of physical limitations and the organic framework within which we function. But this realization will also leave you, or already has, with the indelible and somewhat jarringly ecstatic and frightening notion that there *is* functional truth in the proposition that thought plays a decisive role that is molding, instigative, and formative of your lived experience or conception of reality.

I refer to thought not strictly as a tool of decision, although that too is an aspect of life, but as a galvanic and selective *force*. To assume otherwise is to ascribe too much facility, I think, to the rational, prioritizing facets of intellect, which, experience also teaches, wield so little actual control over the order of life, including our emotions, intimacies, and physically felt urges—much less so control over those of others. And to default to the viewpoint that thought is a limited expression of the physical senses or neuro-system is no longer supportable in our post-materialist era, which we explore in detail in chapter twelve.

To shape a life—and this can creep up on us unawares—is not so much a matter of rational plans, the perception of which we often impose as an illusory order on the past after the fact. Nor is your life wholly the domain of accident since we can divine early in the existence of any individual personality traits that doggedly even deterministically linger. But, rather, life is, in consort with other factors, including some that we cannot gain perspective on, an out-picturing of attitude, hunger, fear, striving, and long-sustained thought. Take this very moment to gaze back on your earliest fantasies, good or ill, or on wishes and fears, passionately harbored during periods of discontent and joy, and see if you do not detect a symmetry.

*   *   *

Can we see reality? Are prejudices hopelessly projected backwards and forwards so that all we see is *expectation*? As alluded earlier, some social scientists (and, more often, science journalists and bloggers) label virtually any personal effort to observe connections between self and the world by the brutally compact term—at once naïve and cynical—confirmation bias. As noted, this is a clinical term for prejudice. We all suffer from it. But to overapply such a judgment to the individual search means limiting questions of emotional and ethical existence to the structures of credentialed study. The overuse of such concepts also means subtly (and futilely) attempting to upend the ageless imperative to *know oneself* in favor of professionally determined protocols of perception. It means indirectly claiming that self-inquiry is illusory outside of licensed probity. From Lao Tzu to Proust to Plath, all is, strictly speaking, mere anecdote, of no greater application to the truth of the human situation than the elections of a subject responding to forced-choice survey questions in a lab or marketing study. (I have observed that some clinical studies, when testing for results in motivation, emotional stimulation, or expectation may, above all, measure the talents of researchers as teachers, guides, or coaches.*)

Yet you know as you are reading these words that you have experienced books, movies, works of art, songs, designs, environments, and testimonies that announce: *I am truth*. And you know "I am truth" by how profoundly *unalone* such a realization makes you feel. So, you also know that I am telling you the truth when I state that

---

* See my *Cosmic Habit Force* and *The Miracle Club*.

life responds to thought as clay to the potter's hand. This response can be difficult to detect in the moment just as you do not now detect the revolving of our planet. It can be subtle, wavelike at first and particulate at a later time. What's more, clay, to continue the metaphor, remains clay. Life as we experience it has limits and requires that we suffer physical laws, which are almost universally felt even if those perceived laws are not ultimate or, for that matter, constant. We will always—but for extremely rare moments—experience mass as density. We will know physical decline. And tactile boundaries. Without structure, we could not, as currently constituted, function or even survive. That is why newness, while necessarily unexpected, reaches us through *familiar* channels. That is why truth announces itself (mostly) without upending agreed upon order, time, space, and mass.

But within the sphere of events in which we function—i.e., our reality—we *are* capable of causation, and, in fact, helpless *not* to engage in causation as we are perpetually thinking, feeling, pondering, and measuring. Hence: be encouraged but also be thoughtful, be watchful, and be careful. Not so careful that you truncate your passions; there is a price paid and good received for everything and this exchange cannot be abrogated. But also not so random that you do not consider fees and measures of outcome.

*   *   *

Given what I have just written, I hope that you will take it very seriously when I ask you: *what do you want?* If you regard that question tritely or abruptly you will either fail to marshal the forces of intent or you will set on a random course—the two outcomes are closely related. At some point in life, this will leave you asking where you went wrong. But if you take that question—*what do you want?*—with deep seriousness, you will be delivered someplace that will, albeit with unforeseen and unexpected details, resemble the molded shape of thought. For this to occur requires patience, intelligent persistence (sometimes called faith), and toleration of discursive terrain. The Western parable of creation occurring over six days followed by a day of rest is, I think, a symbolic representation of the universal fact of mental and creative gestation. We do not know precisely what a "day" represented in the visions of its nameless authors, but nor are we so bound by literalism as to fail to detect a signpost of truth.

And this raises another point of caution. The foundational sources of religion in any society are, as parts of the human striving to know and to record, invariably reflective of truths as they are also reflective of thought models, habits, metaphors, assumptions, and figures of speech of their cultural conveyors. These statements grow overwhelmingly persuasive by dint of repetition, sometimes over the span of millennia. Hence, in Western culture we think of cosmic reality as organized by "higher" (God, heavens) and "lower" (earth, purgatory, underworld). But none of that is an unconditioned truth. Even our measurable physical lives are not governed by the actual existence of up or down. Point "up" right now. That is meaningless to someone a hemisphere away whose experience is every bit as palpable as your own. We know that something called gravity—or what might be considered mass attracted to itself—moors us and our atmosphere to this globe and maintains celestial cycles. But "up" and "down"? Those are figures of speech. Why, then, would such concepts translate to or govern ultimate reality? One could argue that the nature of ultimate reality may transfer to our experience but it is just as likely that we have imposed our perception upon it, and this is probably more provable from the perspective of logic.

In the worldview of Hermeticism—the late ancient Greek-Egyptian philosophy—reality exists in a series of concentric circles emanating from a Great Mind called *Nous*.* As this mind can create, so goes the Hermetic view, your mind can likewise create, albeit within the physical limitations of our concentric circle of existence. I view this as the classical basis of New Thought, although it presents *a parallel, indirect correlation and not a lineage* between the two philosophies. Due to a paucity of translations and the rural environs in which they lived, most

---

* At several points, I refer to the philosophy known since about the mid-seventeenth century as Hermeticism. During the early stages of the Ptolemaic Era (332-30 BC), in which Egypt was dominated by a Greek ruling class descendant from the armies of Alexander, Hellenic philosophers and pedants bestowed on Ancient Egypt's god of writing and intellect Thoth the honorary title Hermes Trismegistus, or thrice-greatest Hermes. This signified the ibis-headed god's superiority to their own deity of communication, Hermes or the later Mercury. For generations, including after the death of Christ, Alexandrian-based Hermetic scribes produced philosophical and magical writings to which they appended the name of Hermes or Hermes Trismegistus; it was a common practice in antiquity to affix the name of a sage or mythical figure to a piece of writing in order to lend it gravity. In these works, later grouped as the Renaissance-era *Corpus Hermeticum* but encompassing of a sprawling range of writings, philosophers posited the existence of an Overmind or *Nous* from which all of humanity emanates. These cosmic scribes saw humanity as projections—which pass through a series of concentric circles or realities—of a great infinite intelligence in which we all participate.

progenitors of New Thought (with the Transcendentalists a notable exception) neither read nor referenced Hermetic literature. Many of their observations were Bible-centered and steeped in individual experiment.

Based on experience and personal study, I embrace the Hermetic view. But, again, generality and figures of thought quickly cloud the picture. I often quote the Hermetic maxim, "As above, so below."* That statement uses the terms I have just called into question. The fact is, some degree of generality or figment of thought (usually consensually agreed to) forms a necessary foundation for communication. But the same figments can also corrupt or limit. This is one of the ways in which paradox is a constant companion on the path and must not be resisted. Truths arrive in polarities. Inability to be at ease with that can drive a seeker to continual frustration.

At age four, I knew that I was different from my playmates—and if you are reading these words, you have probably experienced this, too—when I resisted binary classifications. To cite an explicitly plain but vividly recalled example, when classmates around a kindergarten table feverishly argued over whether Robin is Batman's friend or helper I replied, he is obviously both. Why couldn't they see that?, I wondered. Just as the Joker—

---

* This phrase appears in the late-ancient manuscript called *The Emerald Tablet*. For generations, *The Emerald Tablet* was considered a work of pseudo-Hermeticism crafted in Latin in the medieval era. In the early twentieth century, however, scholars located Arabic versions of *The Emerald Tablet* which date to at least the 700s or 800s AD. This suggests a still-earlier source because much of the original Hermetic literature got preserved in both Greek and Arabic. One of the first English translations of *The Emerald Tablet* comes from Isaac Newton (1642–1727): "*Tis true without lying, certain and most true. That which is below is like that which is above . . .*"

cruel, unpredictable, nihilistic, mirthful—is the necessary opposite that completes Batman's identity. Life is a polarity. I realize that I am practically begging critics to abuse these examples, but they are the truth.

*   *   *

The spiritual or personal search is severely curtailed when we are expected to function within accepted frameworks, repetitions, decisions, and concepts, including those that I posit here. It means that literally no act of verification can be considered appropriate if it diverges from widely recognized—some would say universally validated—statements of truth, which scholars and seekers attempt to fitfully correlate within the folds of humanity's disparate religious literature. Never permit form to dictate result.

One of my frustrations with New Thought is its form. Many of its insights are, in my view, thrilling. This chapter opens with my experiential validation of a basic New Thought theme. That is why I continue to use the term New Thought and value its culture and literature, even as I critique both. But the vessel is flawed. It contains blockages. One of the blockages, I believe, is an understandable but limiting reliance on Judeo-Christian language, formulations, assumptions, and context, as well as on transmuted and popularized Eastern (mostly Buddhist) variants of the same. I once conducted much of my search within those boundaries, especially pertaining to the division of life into a greater unseen world and a temporal fleeting world, and what the experience in each are worth. Yet I came to question those boundaries. Recent to this writing, I had a strange experience. I came across a margin note in a book, which I wrote about ten years earlier with great sincerity and some anguish: "I fear that my ego-hunger for 'success' will overwhelm my search for the higher." I no longer believe in the premises of that statement.

To begin with, notice how "off the shelf" that language is. All of its terminology denotes the assumption that there exists a vaster, below-the-surface (or above-the-surface) life versus an illusory, ego-driven life. Again, I realize how persuasive that framework is. It undergirds much of Western and Eastern religious tradition. But is it true? Does it meet the needs of your insights, experiences, and deepest wishes, not as idealized but as lived? The euphoria experienced in moments of personal victory or sublime self-expression is not to be dismissed. And, of course, the sensation fades. As it should. Expression or attainment is not intended to transfix; it is intended to refine and drive us, just as hunger moves us physiologically.

Experience led me to question the higher-lower, greater-lesser, eternal-temporal paradigm of self-development. Today, I think in terms of self-expression without vertical divisions. There are, as alluded, necessary polarities and graduated states. But where would actual divisions or demarcations begin and end? Where does "ego" turn into something else? When does "essence" flip into "personality?" Or, put differently, dedication into attachment? In any case, these are all metaphors—not fixities of reality or experience.

In matters of the search, actual experience is hard-won. Experience is difficult to honor because it may run counter to longstanding decisions found within spiritual traditions or literature about what is and is not true. Or it may sync with those decisions. The point is: *it must be your own*. An experience can be your own without necessarily being solitary. And this returns me to the formative powers of thought, the note on which I opened this chapter. If I am correct that our experiences are common, consider the extraordinariness of the prospect that *your thoughts are causative*. And the ethical demand that places on you. You possess a wild, ferocious freedom within—which all the more places you before the need to define your principles because you are now, and will continue, living by them with a totality that may not always be clear.

Be *joyful* because a road is open before you. But be deeply *serious* because you are going to experience not only where that road goes but also the personal genesis of the road itself.

Chapter Four

Are We Gods in Our Own Realities?

D o your loved ones, workmates, friends, adversaries, acquaintances, and intimates experience your reality—or their own? Do we share the same world? Or do the infinitude of decisions and outcomes we face produce ever-multiplying and limitless branches of actuality—infinite worlds—which you and I are constantly creating? And if that is so, it means, effectively, that everyone in your world is subject to your perception: you owe them something, as you are owed something.

Each existence, whatever its basis—or its ultimate basis—is valid. If I mistreat another in my realm (an outcome that is nearly impossible to avoid given our lack of perspective, unruliness of emotions, subjective perception of needs, and so on) that implies, as I will argue, a violation that may be felt in another world, if not in this one. Or it may be felt serially. I, too, depend upon others to honor some reciprocal balance with me. In that vein, is

Neville Goddard correct about the godlike status of the lowly seeming and temporarily housed human being?

Let me offer a quantum interlude and then return to this point. I began studying the basics of quantum mechanics in connection with my 2014 book, *One Simple Idea*. I find that restating even the most rudimentary ideas in quantum theory—now generations old—still conveys a sense of revolutionary possibility. We continue to wonder at and debate over the implications and interpretations. In short, more than ninety years of experiments in quantum mechanics demonstrate that atomic-scale particles appear in a given place only after a measurement is made. Quantum theory holds that *no measurement means no precise and localized object* on the atomic level. Put differently, a subatomic particle literally occupies an infinite number of places (a state called "superposition") until observation localizes it in one place. That, at least, is one of the dominant interpretations.

In the parlance of quantum physics, an atomic-scale particle is said to exist in a wave-state, which means that the location of the particle in space-time is known only probabilistically; it has no properties in this state, just potentialities. When particles or waves—typically in the form of a beam of photons or electrons—are directed or aimed at a target system, such as a double-slit, scientists have found that their pattern or path will actually change, or "collapse," depending upon the presence or measurement choices of an observer. Hence, a wave pattern will shift, or collapse, into a particle pattern. Contrary to all reason, quantum theory holds that opposing outcomes simultaneously exist.

The twentieth-century physicist Erwin Schrodinger was frustrated with the evident absurdity of quantum theory, which showed objects simultaneously appearing in more than one place at a time. Such an outlook, he felt, violated all commonly observed physical laws. In 1935, Schrodinger sought to highlight this predicament through a purposely absurdist thought experiment, which he intended to force quantum physicists to follow their data to its ultimate degree.

Schrodinger reasoned that quantum data dictates that a sentient being, such as a cat, can be simultaneously alive and dead. A variant of the "Schrodinger's cat" experiment could be put this way: Let's say a cat is placed into one of a pair of boxes. Along with the cat is what Schrodinger called a "diabolical device." The device, if exposed to an atom, releases a deadly poison. An observer then directs an atom at the boxes. The observer subsequently uses some form of measurement to check on which box the atom is in: the empty one or the one with the cat and the poisoning device. When the observer goes to check, the wave function of the atom—i.e., the state in which it exists in both boxes—collapses into a particle function—i.e., the state in which it is localized to one box. Once the observer takes his measurement, convention says that the cat will be discovered dead or alive. But Schrodinger reasoned that quantum physics describes an outcome in which the cat is *both* dead and alive. This is because the atom, in its wave function, was, at one time, in either box, and either outcome is real.

Of course, all lived experience dictates that if the atom went into the empty box, the cat is alive; and if it went into the box with the cat and the poisoning device, the cat is dead. But Schrodinger, aiming to highlight the frustrations of quantum theory, argued that if the observations of quantum-mechanics experiments are right you would have to allow for each outcome.

To take it even further, a cohort of quantum physicists in the 1950s theorized that if an observer waited some significant length of time, say, eight hours, before checking on the dead-alive cat, he would discover one cat that was dead for eight hours and another that was alive for eight hours (and now hungry). In this line of reasoning, conscious observation effectively manifested the localized atom, the dead cat, the living cat—and *also actualized the past*, i.e., created a history for both a dead cat and a living one. Both outcomes are true.

Consider too: the cat, from its perspective is local; the observer, from its perspective is local—but both are effectively in a wave state or superposition. We can speak of them as concrete, singular beings only from their personal perspective. From the quantum perspective, they are indeterminate or infinite. Expanding on this idea, research physician Robert Lanza, adjunct professor at Wake Forest University School of Medicine, argued that death itself is ultimately a mental phenomenon: we "die" only insofar as the mind perceives demise.

Decades of quantum experiments make this model—in which a being can be dead/alive—into an impossible reality: an unbelievable yet entirely tenable, even necessary state of nature. Schrodinger's thought experiment forced a consideration of the meaning of quantum mechanics.

Further experiments, some of which are already underway, will determine broader implications of micro-cosmic phenomena in the mechanical world in which we live. For now, decades of quantum data make it defensible to reason that observation done on the subatomic scale: 1) shapes the nature of outcomes, 2) determines the presence or absence of a localized object, and 3) possibly devises multiple pasts and presents. This last point is sometimes called the "many-worlds interpretation," in the words of physicist Hugh Everett III. This theory of "many worlds" raises the prospect of an infinite number of realities and states of being, each depending upon our choices.

And here we encounter the alluring, sometimes confounding, but persistent thesis of mind-power metaphysics, which holds that thoughts concretize experience. Everett's concept of multiple worlds and outcomes finds its closest metaphysical analog in the ideas of Neville Goddard.

In an era before the popularization of quantum theory, and before the many-worlds interpretation, Neville commented that we all live in our own dreams of reality which crisscross with one another's. He said this to a lecture audience in Los Angeles in 1948:

Do you realize that no two people live in the same world? We may be together now in this room, but we will go home tonight and close our doors on entirely different worlds. Tomorrow, we will go to work where we'll meet others but each one of us lives in our own mental and physical world.

And later in the same series: "Scientists will one day explain *why* there is a serial universe. But in practice, *how* you use this serial universe to change the future is more important."

Neville meant all of this in the most literal sense. He believed that every individual, possessed of his or her own imagination, is the creative force called God in Scripture, and that everything you encounter, including these words at this instant, is rooted in you, as you are ultimately rooted in the source of creation.

You dwell in a world of infinite possibilities and realities, and, in fact, when you mentally picture something, you are not creating it—it already exists. You are claiming it. The very fact of being able to experience the thing mentally confirms that in this world of infinite possibilities, where imagination is the ultimate creative agent, everything that you can picture *already is*. The teacher further noted:

> Man can prove the existence of a dimensionally larger world by simply focusing his attention on an invisible state and imagining that he sees and feels it. If he remains concentrated in this state, his present environment will pass away, and he will awaken in a dimensionally larger world where the object of his contemplation will be seen as a concrete objective reality.
>
> I feel intuitively that, were he to abstract his thoughts from this dimensionally larger world and retreat still farther within his mind, he would again bring about an externalization of time. He would dis-

cover that, every time he retreats into his inner mind and brings about an externalization of time, space becomes dimensionally larger. And he would therefore conclude that both time and space are serial, and that the drama of life is but the climbing of a multitudinous dimensional time block.

Aleister Crowley, the confounding and brilliant British occultist and artist, made a statement related to Neville's. Writing in the introduction to his 1904 channeled text *The Book of the Law*—later published in a general edition in 1938—Crowley observed:

> Each of us has thus an universe of his own, but it is the same universe for each one as soon as it includes all possible experience. This implies the extension of consciousness to include all other consciousnesses. In our present stage, the object that you see is never the same as the one that I see; we infer that it is the same because your experience tallies with mine on so many points that the actual differences of our observation are negligible . . . Yet all the time neither of us can know anything . . . at all beyond the total impression made on our respective minds.

So how does that weigh upon your experience of other people? Are others "real"—or are they projected concepts of your perspective and emotionalized thoughts?

Seen from one vantage point, it must be said that others are entirely real. You confront this reality, jarringly and not infrequently, when you attempt to change someone. It is nearly impossible. Few things have caused greater tragedy and frustration across myriad lives than vain efforts to bend another person to your will, even if there are sound reasons, such as overcoming addiction or improving work habits or providing you or another with due consideration.

At the same time, I do believe that others *are* framed and affected in our realities by thought causation—while simultaneously possessing their own independent and objectively real existence. It is wholly possible, even necessary, that our activities reverberate in myriad ways across unending dimensions, which reflect infinite paths and behaviors taken and untaken. The proverbial cat in the quantum-physics thought experiment is logically demonstrated to be both alive and dead because experiments involving subatomic particles prove that multiple outcomes can—and must—coexist based on the decision of an observer. Hence, your life and experience at this moment may reflect accumulated possibilities and reciprocities that play out in serial realities of which you are a part but are not necessarily aware at a given instance of perception. The noisy neighbor who disturbs you, the lover who understands you, the child who alternately evokes affection and anger in you—all of them may be reflective of myriad interdimensional processes and actions on your part and that of others. This is, perhaps, why people seem at once impossible to change and yet also deeply affected by your intentions, even (or especially) when unspoken.

The question of whether your relations are perfectible, and all the more so whether the events you witness around you are perfectible, is determined by vast and intersecting realities. Neville promises that *the world is as you are.* I consider that true. At the same time, the "you" in question may be an infinitude of existences, thus making the task of interpersonal and self-creation appear at once tantalizingly intimate and possible and, by turns, faraway and impossibly frustrating. That is the paradox of our creative-mind reality.

In the philosophy of Hermeticism, the human is viewed as superior to the gods because he or she is always in the act of *becoming*—of progressing into greater states. The gods possess one immortal existence; but the individual leads *both* mortal and immortal existences, which may also be seen as a metaphor for multiple lives. Hence, "ye are gods," as Psalm 82 says, but we are flawed gods, because we must contend not only with the physical limitations of our mortal lives but also with the multiple and unintended effects of lives conducted within endless realities.

Given the vastness of these influences, are we effectively subject to randomness? Is self-willed mind metaphysics fruitless? I believe it is not. But what I have been describing may lay behind the often-laborious schemes of unfoldment that our wishes—and nightmares—assume. I contend that those thought patterns most capable of concretizing experience, like signals amid the noise of myriad influences and events, are your most intimately felt and persistently held images of self, often extending back to earliest childhood and presently intact in ways that you may not always suspect. Are you aware of these self-conceptions and images? This is why a clarified aim is so critical.

Allow your aim to shape the internal image, at every moment possible, of your lived existence. Use every means to populate your psyche with this self-image. This image is the psycho-spiritual equivalent of the Tree of Knowledge of Good and Evil (perhaps simultaneously the Tree of Life) from which Eve ate and came into awareness—and also friction. It is the tree we have been conditioned not to touch; to avoid in favor of eternal childhood, with its dependency and safety (at least as idealized); but it is also the fruit we must consume—*our self-created image*—in order to fulfill the potential indicated in Hermetic literature: that of a being engaged in the act of *becoming*, across all intersecting realities.

So which reality—if indeed one—are you living from right now? We turn next to that question.

Chapter Five

Time Travel

Neville observed that forgiveness is revision. In an exercise he called "the pruning shears of revision," the mystic prescribed mentally reexperiencing a regrettable event—whether bad news, an unhappy episode, a personal confrontation—in the manner in which *you wish* it had occurred. Neville once said that he believed this method was the insight for which he would be most widely remembered.

I have sometimes looked askance at this exercise. I have found that the passions associated with friction are at times too great for me to sustain "revision" of a scene in my imagination. Moreover, I am not always certain that I *want* revision. I sometimes desire victory in a given circumstance rather than refinement of it. But there are also moments when life provides an opening that beckons us to try a new approach or reattempt an old one. Recent to this writing, I had one such experience. It bore powerful fruit.

One rainy day, I was delivering a live talk via Zoom to a convention of New Thought practitioners and ministers in the Midwest. My energy was low and I was fatigued from successfully but arduously reaching the finish line on a range of projects, which became due at roughly the same time. The talk went fine. But it started off a little slowly, my thoughts were a bit scattered (I frankly could have prepared more), and, while the momentum picked up to a successful midpoint and conclusion, I did not feel that it was one of my finest presentations. I felt rueful about this because I always like to deliver my best work to an audience. I was being paid and I felt an obligation in that regard, too. I recorded the talk—and when watching back the opening minutes, I experienced pangs of regret.

I entered a state of meditation and decided to "revise" the episode according to Neville's approach. I ran a scene through my head, seeing myself concluding an effective and polished talk. When I emerged, I found myself feeling better about the presentation. I viewed the video opening again and it seemed more supple and complete. Not necessarily perfect by my lights—but significantly more natural and satisfying. It seemed more like me. Having already received the host's permission, I decided to post the talk on YouTube. I had not posted public content there in a while and it seemed like a propitious opportunity.

The following morning, I continued my thought exercise. I woke up and sat in meditation (my personal method is Transcendental Meditation) and then ran through my head a small scene of the talk proceeding deftly. A realization hit me. I owed another organization a description for an upcoming presentation. The group for which I just delivered my talk had, for reasons of technicality, not used the promotional copy and description

I had sent them. Since I was planning to consider similar themes for this other event—this was a gratis talk for a research-based organization—I had the opportunity to use my unseen description anew. It was a "second chance" to deliver the talk; it was a fresh approach to the past in the now.

And what of the talk I had just delivered? How did my efforts at "revision" go? I am about to present an excerpt from it. It is a passage that I delivered without foresight of writing this chapter, but the passage reflects upon what may be *happening* when we practice revision. Immediately following the excerpt, I provide two candid reactions, one from a viewer and the other from my host, both of which arrived subsequent to the exercises that I have just described.

My contention is that even if awareness or consciousness is the ultimate arbiter of existence, we still experience many different laws and forces within the physical framework that we occupy. I used to say that we *live* under many different laws and forces; I'm not sure if that's entirely right. But we certainly *experience* many different laws and forces, and these experiences are very hard baked into us. So, it stands to reason that even if emotive thought, perspective, and awareness are determinative of what reality gets concretized into our individual experiences, there are different laws and possibilities that are also playing out at the same time. There are physical facts which also form part of the nature of our experience within this framework that we find ourselves. And it could be that there are other frameworks in which our psyches are much freer. It could be that there are other frameworks in which we experience *fewer* laws and forces that seem to interrupt a sense of continuity between you the individual, you the seeker, and that which you experience.

Within string theory, a term that's commonly heard nowadays, there exists a theorized model of reality in which all of life, all that is, exists along these kinds of vibrating strings. And every particle, every universe, everything that's experienced, is connected through these vibrating strings so that all the potential realities that I've been talking about exist, but they exist perhaps out of sight or out of experience from the individual. The individual experiences usually one reality going on at a time but there are these different realities and possibilities along these so-called vibrating strings. At least that's one iteration of string theory.

Let me interject into this a theory and a possibility. We're living through a moment in the twenty-first century where there exists the most concrete visual evidence a person could ask for with respect to UFO phenomena; for example, we have evidence on high-definition video from Navy fighter-pilot cockpits; we have evidence on radar; we have the Pentagon releasing a report referencing nearly 150 cases, saying that these are things that we've documented and made inquiries over, and we're experiencing forms of technology that are not explicable by any worldly understanding that we possess.

So, we have confirmation of the existence of UFOs as a question that goes outside of any of the ordinary categories that we may have grown up with. When I was a kid, if you talked about UFOs somebody would always say, "swamp gas, weather balloon, illusion, imagination, little green men," and blah, blah, blah. Those dismissals seem like they belong to yesterday. No serious person nowadays would dispute the validity of the UFO thesis. And one of the things that has occurred to me is that given the theoretical models that we have, it may be easier to explain the UFO thesis by interdimensionality than by figuring out ways that such vast distances in our galaxy or our universe could be spanned by physical craft. It's a greater theoretical problem to try to figure out how a physical craft could attain interstellar travel than it is to rely upon quantum mechanical and string theory models. And to ask the question, "Is it possible that, from time to time, those of us occupying this dimension that we more or less consensually agree upon, experience stuff that's going on in other dimensions?" We then give it names like extraterrestrial or Bigfoot or the Loch Ness monster or ghosts or poltergeists. We have testimonies that go back to time immemorial that are remarkably and tantalizingly consistent. And now, in 2021 we have theoretical models that seriously posit the possibility, maybe even the necessity, of the existence of other dimensions.

We have data for the extra-physical and the causal factors of the mind; we have these accounts of so-called UFOs that are more vivid and more validated now than any time in human history; and it could be that we right now in 2021 are getting better glimpses of what it means to be multi-dimensional beings, of what it means for the psyche possibly to be multi-dimensional and infinite, than we as a human species have understood at any time in the past. And there's a long way to go until those doors of perception are cleansed. If I'm on the right trail—I don't know that I am but it falls to every generation to at least try to understand what's around the next corner—it could be that our generation is experiencing an opening that will ultimately result in a redefinition of human nature at least as much as the advent of Darwin's theory of evolution resulted in a redefinition of human nature in the Victorian era. And we may be just at the beginning, just at the infancy, of starting to understand ourselves as multi-dimensional beings, as beings possessed of psyches that are infinite.

And it's difficult, because, of course, one of the things that we must contend with, as well, is the absolute reality of physical decline and demise. These bodies that we're in are going to decay. We're going to experience, every one of us, decline and demise as traditionally understood in our world. And yet, the very opening to the possibility of physical non-locality does begin to leaven even the question of the ultimate nature of death. Of course, seekers have been probing the question of the psychical survival of death for millennia, so this is nothing new; but what's new, I think, is that we're seeing a convergence of understandings, a convergence of conversations, a convergence of possibilities; and it's strange because we live in a world that politically and culturally is so divided, and yet at the same time we are starting to see a convergence between the probing and experiments going on within the theoretical and hard sciences and the probing and experiments going on among everyday seekers. For all of the fraying in our world, there's no question that those conversations are starting to come together. The question for us as seekers is, what do we do with this information?

A viewer, Genifer Halisky, wrote on Twitter: "Managed to sit and focus on this for an hour. If you can make me grasp string theory, you can teach me anything @MitchHorowitz. Bravo. [clapping hands emoji] Quite enjoyed this one." And what did the original host think? A week after I delivered my talk, the organization sent me—wholly unexpectedly (and without precedent)—a bouquet of flowers. It appears here:

Those gratifying responses were the furthest I could have imagined before attempting the pruning-shears exercise. Did my talk "change"—or did my perception of it change? Or did both occur? I am an experienced speaker and I usually have a reasonable assessment of how a presentation went. That the responses surprised me coincided with my own psychical shift following the exercises.

*   *   *

Let me revisit the question of method and its implications. I happened upon a useful "pruning" technique one day while meditating. It related to a different situation, one from years earlier, which I hungered to emotionally revise. In short, I hurt another person with my words and I wanted to undo the harm that I caused. I had often thought of the circumstance but experienced difficulty revising the scene in a wholly persuasive, satisfying manner. Returning to it, however, I now reimagined just *one element* of the scene; and in my mind, I intentionally *slowed down* this revised moment—as though reducing the speed of a video—so that a very brief exchange was re-experienced at a detailed and deliberate pace, with each moment pronounced. For example, imagine saying "good morning" to someone but with the exchange slowed frame-by-frame and the language itself decelerated to a drawl, so that every element of the episode becomes apparent. I repeated this approach three times in one sitting. I felt awash in relief each time I did it. There is no limit to the number of times you can try this technique or return to it across different sessions.

I used to wonder if Neville's method of "changing the past" could hypothetically result in jarring or even unwanted change in the present. Isn't that the traditional or popularized view of "time travel?" Changing one element changes them all, quite possibly with harrowing and unpredictable results. But perhaps that is not how revision works. What if the antecedent event and its alternative proceed in real but different dimensions? The thing that gets altered forms a new dimensional strand or string—imagine reality as an endlessly expansive ball of twine—and the "anchor strand" from which you reconceived the event remains circumstantially untouched. What *is* touched, what is altered, is the emotional antecedent of the incident. So that your anchor reality and the psyches of those you encounter within it—independent beings who crisscross from time to time within your perception of reality or intertwined strings, as you do within theirs—are leavened by the alteration of experience with the perceived event unchanged.

Hence, if you look at a piece of evidence from the past, such as an email, it may reflect the incident. The current reality bears its forensic markings. (In chapter three, I wrote, "truth announces itself (mostly) without upending agreed upon order, time, space, and mass.") But because you wove a different strand—you selected a different dimensional storyline to experience and thus launched another among infinite serial worlds—there exists a kind of ripple effect in which salvific effects are felt in the anchor point. There is also, by this logic, an alternative reality—one among an infinite number—where altered circumstance, jarring or salving, is experienced. Within the anchor reality of your inceptive thought point, the emotive ripple is felt. Healing can occur. The opposite is also true, so we should be careful when we consider the question of reviewing the past or when we idly revise or rerun its scenes.

And what of concrete changes to events themselves? I cited the example of delivering a talk that I considered below par. After "revision," I posted the talk and received plaudits from both new viewers and from the original host. Allowing for the possibilities that I have just referenced, did the event change within my inceptive framework? Or am I perhaps writing these words from a *different reality* to which the new event now belongs? Have I, through confidence of perception and emotional willingness, elected to live from a different perspective, which is to say a different dimension? Perhaps the dimension in which the original event occurred is forensically unchanged—but I, as the observer, have "leaped" to a new point of experience along the intersecting strings of reality.

As alluded earlier, from the perspective of the figures in the Schrodinger's cat experiment—the observer and the cat—they are singular, local, and concrete. But quantum laws dictate that this is just a point of view. In actuality, these figures, beyond their personal perspective, are multi-dimensional. As are you and me.

*   *   *

I mentioned the factor of emotional willingness. The lever of this exercise—as well as a potential barrier—is the *authenticity of wanting*. Nothing else brings convictive clarity. As noted, Neville equated revision with forgiveness. In Neville's mystical reading of Scripture, to forgive does not mean to excuse but to *re-vision* an adversary or fractious encounter according to your ideal. As suggested earlier, I am not always emotionally or ethically certain that I truly *want* to undo or reverse an event so much as resolve it on my own terms. This is a fact of human nature with which we must honestly reckon. Do you want peace—or victory? Is one exclusive of the other? Our emotions always pull us in the direction of authentic desire. Our inner or outer voices may conceal our motives; our emotions expose them.

I believe that there are periods in which we actually want to hang onto negative situations, themes, or memories. For example, a perceived adversary may also be someone for whom you harbor deep feelings, even love. What is love but the opposing polarity of hate? In both situations, another person shapes, marks, and even gives direction or purpose to one's life. We often see love and hate as opposites but, in a sense, they are the same rhythmical continuum, a point on which I expand in the next chapter.

Hence, we may wish, without ever fully expressing it to ourselves, to retain, review, repeat, and even re-live a difficulty. That dynamic may also occur because the problematic situation afforded us no emotional closure and we continually rerun it in search of resolve. Closure is a subjective feeling that arises from exiting a situation with some personally conceived degree of dignity, approval, or maturity. It is a restoration of one's sense of self, accurate or not. Other times, we may savor or enjoy conflict, which might provide a feeling of *aliveness* or a thrill of having escaped. An attachment could present us with a bevy of variegated or conflicting emotions ranging from fear to allure. Fear and allure are also part of the same continuum. Finally, a trauma cycle may involve feelings of deep injustice, which we fitfully, and often unconvincingly, use our imaginations to try and fix or restore. This can lead to "what ifs?" in which we may repeatedly imagine telling someone off or rescuing ourselves from trouble through foresight or a quick response.

None of what I just described is *revision* in the manner defined by Neville. But nor am I exactly criticizing the approaches that I have referenced. A wise man once said that justice is nothing but a mental idea; that is, a necessarily limited or peripherally blind perspective on a situation based on selfishness or boundaries of perception. I have lived with that statement for years. I am unsure it is correct, at least as an absolute. I believe that the mature individual possesses a valid scale of reference for how he or she is treated in life, and likewise has some conception of just and unjust scenarios pertaining to the autonomy of his or her psyche and body.

In that vein, I once knew the cofounder of a New Age center who I personally considered pompous. He threw his opinions and his weight around knowing that few people would counter him since he occupied a position of influence at a prominent growth center. After many years of our being out of touch, I received an email from him chiding me for something I had written in the ideas section of a newspaper. His objection was due to an obvious misreading of my point. I plainly said so, consequences be damned. In replying bluntly to someone who often abused people's indulgence with ersatz parables of wisdom or discursive stories pointing to the listener's faults, I experienced a wave of relief. After years of biting my tongue, I responded to this man in a manner that few seemed willing to. The ensuing feeling of peace, of a wrong relationship set aright, never left me. I consider that some modicum of justice. Perhaps I was not an independent actor. Perhaps I only functioned as a passive agent of natural reciprocity or what is sometimes called karma.

From the perspective of larger currents of reciprocity, an event may occur that slakes our thirst for justice, albeit indirectly. This may be what Nietzsche had in mind when he wrote in *Beyond Good and Evil* in 1886: "One *has* to repay good and ill—but why precisely to the person who has done us good or ill?" (From the 1966 Kaufmann translation.) This is a disquieting principle. Why should payment be extracted from an uninvolved pedestrian? To this objection the philosopher might reply: why then should good tidings be granted to any such person?— as in the popular concept of "pay it forward." Perhaps *both* consequences are unwarranted on an intimate scale but arise from matters other than the one immediately perceived. Nietzsche's ideal may reflect the impersonal scales of life found within concepts of karma in Vedic theology. Within traditional Hinduism and Buddhism, karmic balances of equilibrium are unseeable and ineffable, not infrequently harsh, and spread across vast reaches of time. In that vein, I might reframe the philosopher's statement from "one *has* to repay" to "nature *has* to repay."

Both Nietzsche and the wise man I quoted earlier remind me that I must bow to the limits of perspective. What do I know of my interlocutor's family background or personal circumstances? What do I know of the antecedents for his behavior? Someone once wrote me a brutally critical letter damning me for every aspect of my life and behavior. What the correspondent did not realize was that I had spent several months crying myself to sleep and hoarsening my throat in prayer because of a personal failing to which the letter referred. If the writer could have seen that background, it might have changed things. I do not know. So, I must also be clear that, although I argue for justice and injustice as detectable polarities, I recognize how susceptible such views are to circumstance.

What I *can* conclude is that the effectiveness of Neville's pruning-shears approach rests upon the *authenticity and emotional clarity* of the individual's wish to undo, and hence idealize, a situation. This is why, again and again, I insist upon self-honesty. It is the solution upon which every choice and possibility rests, at least insofar as we are independent beings.

*   *   *

Let me offer a not-quite-final word about time and non-linearity with particular reference to the title of this book. Artist and musician Michael Nesmith of the Monkees made an intriguing observation in his 2017 memoir *Infinite Tuesday*: "One continuously positive idea I've carried from my early years is an ever-expanding notion that the past does not create the present—that what seems set in perpetuity can be instantly changed. This was never an argument for randomness, but more of a sense of an eternal present that was constantly updating, revealing more and more of the moments that comprised infinite Life." Nesmith, who passed away recent to this writing, grew up within the metaphysical faith of Christian Science; his reflection could have come from the pen of Neville Goddard.

The title of this book, *Daydream Believer*, is, of course, inspired by the Monkees' 1967 hit, a song as anthemic and memorable as anything to reach number-one on the pop charts. Written by singer-songwriter John Stewart (formerly of the Kingston Trio) and performed by Monkees vocalist Davy Jones (all of the band members play on the track), the song "Daydream Believer" is actually darker than its reputation as a paean to fairytale love come true.

In a 2006 interview with the Archives of Music Preservation, Stewart explained that he wrote the song as the third of a "suburbia trilogy" about tarnished dreams and, specific to "Daydream Believer," love dulled by domestic tedium. Stewart's meaning, however, got altered by a word change. The famous lyrics go: "You once thought of me/ As a white knight on his steed/ Now, you know how happy I can be." As originally written, however, the line went: "Now you know how *funky* I can be." RCA Records insisted on changing "funky" to "happy." Although the term funky later came to be associated with R&B dance music and disco-era street culture, its former meaning indicated something oily, greasy, or even rancid, as in a "funky odor." The Monkees had already landed hits with dark lyrical undercurrents, such as "I'm Not Your Stepping Stone" (a slap at social climbing), "Last Train to Clarksville" (a subtle anti-Vietnam anthem), and "Pleasant Valley Sunday " (an x-ray of suburban dystopia). But no way were the hitmakers at RCA going to allow the cherubic Davy to sing the lyric "funky." Hence, with a single word change, the tenor of the worldwide hit went from wistful to idyllic.

In using the title *Daydream Believer,* I am honoring a band that I love—and with which I have had strange, albeit indirect, associations. I am also acknowledging what I hope is a core point of this book: that the powers of thought causation, while entirely real, are not an exit ramp from the frictions, challenges, and caprices of life. If you hunger for an existence of Edenic monotony, this book is not for you.

I mentioned my odd entanglement with the Monkees. In the summer of 2016, for no apparent reason I began diving deep into the Monkees' discography and reading histories of the band. I wrote about the Monkees in my manuscript-in-progress for *The Miracle of a Definite Chief Aim,* extolling them as an example of how commercial success can, if deftly handled, translate into artistic clout, allowing the packaged band to finally, if briefly, write and play its own music. Into the winter of 2016, my Monkee-mania burned unabated. At that time, I was surprised to receive a phone call from a culture editor at *The Washington Post* asking if I knew that Mike Nesmith was into Christian Science. No, I said. Would I like to review Nesmith's new memoir, *Infinite Tuesday*? Of course. Did I know or have any connection to Nesmith? No. But—how odd: for months previously, without any foreknowledge,

I had been immersing myself in the Monkees' music and backstory. These events had the same feeling of a time collapse to which Nesmith referred and I explore on my own terms in *The Miracle Club*.

In my review of Nesmith's memoir, I wrote, "He is right: reality doesn't travel straight lines. Months before being asked to review Nesmith's book, with no awareness of its publication or any correlation, I developed a renewed attachment to the Monkees." I called it an example of what the author meant by "Infinite Tuesday"—a nonlinear realm of infinite, coexisting events. Three years later, I had the opportunity to say hello to Monkees' lead singer Micky Dolenz, who I spotted standing alone at an airport in Kansas City. As we spoke, he stared searchingly into my face as though to ask, "Do I know you?"

Chapter Six

Why Prayer Works

The notion of prayer can sound quaint, tame, or overly familiar, especially to people concerned with magickal operations. But I believe, above all, in simplicity and power. And prayer is an extraordinary means of employing the extra-physical. Provided you do not get trapped by form.

Throughout this book, I try to squarely face the reality that, at times, talk of employing the agencies of the mind can seem frustrating or futile when one feels crushed by the difficulties of life. There are episodes or extended periods when all of us feel defeated by personal crisis, financial need, depression, disappointment, or sorrow. When physical or emotional pain, loss, grief, or the burdens of daily existence lock us in a grip, what should we do from the perspective of esoteric spirituality?

Before I enter into the question of prayer, let me note an insight that spans Hermeticism and Transcendentalism; it might be called the law of rhythm. You can rely on the fact that pendulum swings are inherent to life.

Ralph Waldo Emerson's 1841 essay "Compensation" discusses the cyclical ebb and flow of existence and how every loss or gap is cyclically redressed: "If you serve an ungrateful master, serve him the more. Put God in your debt. Every stroke shall be repaid. The longer the payment is withholden, the better for you; for compound interest on compound interest is the rate and usage of this exchequer."

The ever-morphing nature of life does not mean an absence of symmetry: the swing of a pendulum in one direction is necessarily mirrored by its swing to the other. Isaac Newton likewise observed that objects, both micro and macro, relatively near and unfathomably far, mirror one another's motion. I believe this law holds true on the psychological and event-based plane. Hence, when you are suffering, an inevitable counter swing or mirror motion will, in the near or long term, provide respite. Your moods, enthusiasms, and mental states are part of this lawful mirror-swing.*

There may be times when that pendulum swing seems very far off. At 4 a.m. when you cannot sleep, talk of pendulum swings is not a warming sensation. This returns me to prayer. I feel strongly that when nothing else delivers us, *appeals and petitions can be made to greater forces.* I believe that prayer and petitions to a deific entity, infinite mind, or greater force represents an authentic and potent possibility. I am not talking about just one kind of prayer or a form of prayer that necessarily fits within our mono-

---

* This is not to discount chronic emotional suffering. In that vein, I have included an appendix, "Depression and Metaphysics."

theistic worldview or sees greater powers as figments of thought.

I invite you to consider: What if our ancient, pantheistic ancestors—whose lives and civilizations spanned the globe for millennia and laid the foundation for our present—were religiously insightful? They were right about many things, from calendrics to geometry to agriculture to architecture to the rudiments of civil law. I recall weeping when I discovered that ancient people who occupied the Negev Desert about 25,000 years ago created an altar to worship the moon. I was profoundly moved by this because it reflected early humanity's effort to identify something greater than itself; to vest its existence in more than hunt, harvest, and reproduction; to seek connection with the cosmic. Much like Eve biting the apple, it made humanity itself.

As time passed, from the Indus Valley to Siberia to Polynesia, all ancient people—with remarkable consistency and archetypal symmetry—brought a sense of personification to the energies and cycles that they detected in nature. Their understanding of nature—a requisite of survival and sustenance in a world where death formed a palpable presence—ran much deeper than our own. The ancients often imbued these energies with traits, personas, and deific qualities; they sought relationships with them, including of a petitionary nature. They made vows and offerings (sometimes symbolically, sometimes literally) in exchange for favors requested. Entire systems of civilization developed around these structures. Without calendars, currency, spirituality, and ceremony, early civilization would not have taken shape.

I cautioned, however, not to get trapped by form in matters of prayer. I do not personally believe that dramatic or rote systems—including hierarchies or protracted and rehearsed liturgies—are necessary to reach greater forces. Why would they be? In matters of prayer, I am again guided by the Hermetic principle: *as above, so below*. The same qualities necessary for a transcendent relationship are those required for any mature relationship: affinity, empathy, insight, seriousness, sincerity, clarity, and respect.

In many regards, your temple is your psyche. The greatest gift that the alternative spiritual culture has granted our age, since its stirrings in the Romantic era and then in transcendentalist movements and occult revivals of the mid-to-late nineteenth century, is the rebirth of the insight, once held within Neoplatonic and Hermetic movements, that the psyche is a medium of exchange between the individual and the liminal. The psyche forms a tissue of connection between the psychological and the transcendent or numinous.

Of course, some modern occult movements embrace or reembrace ceremonial structure. If that works for an individual or group, just as congregational spirituality plays an important role for some seekers, I applaud it. But it is not my way. I realized in my early thirties that the congregational model, whether involving the traditional Judaism of my youth or metaphysical ceremonies in which I later joined, were not vehicles of inspiration for me.

Today, I pursue a relationship with greater forces based on historical and personal affinity. When the Ancient Greeks encountered Egypt's god of wisdom,

Thoth, they fell to their knees in awe; they honored him as "thrice greatest" their own Hermes, hence the honorific title *Hermes Trismegistus*, the mythic being at the heart of Hermetic philosophy. Did they experience authentic insight? I am unprepared to say they did not. That encounter, which helped shape our modern language, intellect, science, and broadly defined conceptions of commerce, altered the world we occupy. Who am I to conclude that the Ancient Egyptians, whose empire existed for thousands of years—for centuries longer than what we call Western civilization—were existentially wrong? When Greek historian Herodotus (484–425 BC) encountered the pyramids, those monuments were as ancient to him as he is to us. Who am I to venture that this empire, which underwent changes and alterations as well as consistencies across millennia, had a misconception of greater forces?

*   *   *

Try this as a thought experiment. Consider whether the ancient gods have been neglected. What if they hunger for your attention? What if they long for veneration in a world that has largely forgotten them? Can gods be lonely?

Well, if one conceives of greater intelligences, it stands to reason that empathy, too, must be present within an intelligence. Without empathy one being cannot fully understand another. Empathy is based in the emotions. The finer your emotions, the more keenly developed your sense of empathy and overall ethics. All-seeing beings, or at least beings with greater perspective, must have an expansively greater capacity for empathy. This may be why spiritual philosopher G.I. Gurdjieff spoke of humanity's role as relieving the suffering of God. A teacher once told me that seekers often believe that attaining some degree of spiritual development means that they are going to be happier. But will a person be happier if he or she feels more and more of what is going on in the lives of surrounding beings?

If deific or energetic intelligences experience intensely felt emotions, that may also explain why the pantheon of gods, from ancient Africa to Iceland, often appear in parables and stories as possessing fallible, sometimes frustratingly human traits, including jealousy, rage, fickleness, and lust. Hence, I would venture that, yes, the old gods may be lonely.

In that vein, read the late-ancient Hermetic work *Asclepius*, a beautiful, bittersweet dialogue that accurately prophesied the decline of Egypt and its pantheon. Or read other statements of ancient devotion, such as the *Orphic Hymns*. *Asclepius* not only prophesies the Hermetic world's decline but also its rebirth. Moreover, the dialogue asserts that the individual, in his or her reverence and worship, performs necessary acts of caretaking of the gods: "He not only advances toward god; he also makes the gods strong."* William James made a similar observation in his essay "Is Life Worth Living?" in 1895: "I confess that I do not see why the very existence of an invisible world may not in part depend on the personal response which

---

* I am quoting from—and heartily recommend—Brian P. Copenhaver's *Hermetica* (Cambridge University Press, 1992).

any one of us may make to the religious appeal. God himself, in short, may draw vital strength and increase of very being from our fidelity."

Within these observations appears a bridge between the notion that "all is mind" versus the idea of an outside deity. If one follows the reasoning of the Hermeticists and James, there is symbiosis, wholeness, oneness. Albeit there may exist feelings of difference between self and deity. These impressions, possibly a mental construct, may themselves narrow as the individual develops a sense of familiarity, even if fleeting and incomplete, with his or her own metaphysical existence and proportions. This does not mean that the branch and the tree are the same thing. I *do* believe that deific entities are actual and possess a spectrum of traits; I do not believe that they are simply a projection or variant of thought. I do not consider it "cheating" in matters of transcendence if we both pray and, say, subscribe to Neville Goddard's outlook of mind as creator. Whitman: "(I am large, I contain multitudes.)"

What if by reaching out to the gods, you find yourself in the position of giving hallowed comfort to an ancient entity or energy? If you are moved by this idea, and if you take seriously the notion of personal revelation, then along with what we have been considering, make a plea to the ancients. I propose that you settle into a quiet or meditative mood tonight—or right now—with these principles in mind. Make a direct appeal to whatever deity you feel sympathetic toward. See what happens. Try it as a personal experiment. You are reading this book because you are interested in experiential spiritual philosophy. Now, if what I am describing sounds foolish to you, do not do it.

Do not waste your time. But I am a seeker. As such, I try. I offer my own personal example shortly.

*   *   *

So, what happens when you pray? Well sometimes, seemingly, nothing. But I have experienced indelibly felt results—sometimes quickly. Emotional conviction can, of course, be exceedingly persuasive. Emotions form memories. That is why people raised in the same household often have different perspectives on or recollections of what occurred: we recall what we *feel*. Indifference often means a lack of long-term memory retention. Hence, events are likely to be recorded based on emotional stake. Seen in that light, social scientists might say that someone like me fails to recall the times when prayers are not "answered." And yet, the apparent absence of an answer has often proven extraordinary. I am struck by the protection afforded by *not* attaining things I wanted—and that would have harmed or destroyed me.

For example, in spring 2006 I visited the offices of a publishing company that I long admired. The company had a new corporate owner and I felt certain that I had a vision for how to keep it successful in a shifting media landscape. I wanted to become an executive there, possibly editor-in-chief. The president welcomed me into his office. We spent a friendly and encouraging morning together. Afterward, I had lunch with a childhood friend who worked there. "You're not gonna like this place," he told me. "We have metal desks." Metal desks. The smell of ink from the adjoining warehouse. A quirky and curious backlist. To me, it was like Valhalla. My spirits ran high for days after.

But I got nowhere. I soon discovered that the president who nicely welcomed me into his office swiped some of my book ideas. (As did his short-lived successor, believe it or not.) I am open about ideas. I share them. That sometimes means getting burned. But rarely to any avail. As it happened, the new corporate owner had no idea what to do with the place. They made leaky investments. They made decisions that jeopardized the eclectic and free-wheeling nature of the list. Then the 2008 recession hit. Tragically, layoffs began. Today, the once-storied publishing company is a shell of what it was. Had I received what I wanted and prayed for—namely, a leading executive role—I would have ended up presiding over a funeral. I would have spent my Friday afternoons laying off workers rather than publishing, editing, and writing.

In a twist, I soon became editor-in-chief of the imprint I was already at and did many of the things that I would have done if I had gone to the other company. (And I am proud to say that not one person at my imprint got laid off during the 2008 recession, which saw the closure of the national book chain Borders.) Even the sticky-fingered presidents of the other place inadvertently helped me: their knockoffs of my public-domain editions clarified some tangential copyright issues. And, most important of all, in fall of that year I sold the proposal for my first book, *Occult America*. Had I landed my "dream job," I would not have had adequate time to dedicate myself to the writing and media that followed. I probably would not be writing this book now.

By not receiving what I prayed and hungered for, I was rescued. This has happened to me many times, and probably to you, often with the same eventual flood of palpable relief. Such episodes make me reflect on the epigraph that writer Truman Capote (1924–1984) attributed to Saint Teresa of Avila in his final (and, ironically, unfinished) novel, *Answered Prayers*: "More tears are shed over answered prayers than unanswered ones." Capote was, in a sense, a case study of his point. The brilliant stylist and razor-tongued raconteur attained fame after the 1966 publication of his literary-journalistic classic *In Cold Blood*. Parties, TV engagements, nights out, travel, and champagne and drugs flowed. So much so, that Capote seemed to eventually neglect the task of being a working writer. The onetime literary wonder was transformed into an arriviste. Capote received everything he wanted—and it likely destroyed him. The heavy-drinker's once-cherubic features prematurely aged. Capote died of liver damage and drug toxicity a month before his sixtieth birthday, his last novel incomplete.

I often wonder whether there is an invisible protection in unanswered prayers—as painful as the sense of loss can at first feel. In full disclosure—and I have always vowed to be frank about my search—I am writing this book with a sense of melancholy. I am experiencing, as I write these words, a paucity of hoped-for progress in certain areas of my work. I have a ground rule. I will not work with cynical or dishonest people. Hence, I have had to sustain certain losses by walking away from compromised projects or alliances. Doing so has brought pain. Not regret, but sorrow. I would be betraying your trust if I avoided this topic while writing an avowedly blunt book, or if I rushed to paper over hard experiences with "lessons learned."

As of this writing, I am in a state of questioning. I have prayed from this state. I have been reminded of the certainty I felt earlier toward the publishing job from which I was rescued. I have been reminded of the vastness of achievement that I have experienced from, say, just five years, or even one year, earlier. Prayer is, in a sense, a disclosure. It may grant. It may protect. But it always tells us *what is*. And not infrequently what will be. Prayer opens the folds of your psyche *where you already hold the answer*. That is the truth of any system of divination or appeal to greater forces: *we know the answer*. Various methods reprocess the answer to us in ways that we are capable of absorbing. That is why messages from astrological analyses, Tarot spreads, or consultations with seemingly talented channelers can reach us with the quality of familiarity. We recognize ourselves within them—yet credit the outside source.

That does not necessarily mean that such methods do not also contain objective and valid information. You will recall what I noted about the need to sustain paradox.

Divinatory methods or their messengers can be wrong, too. Years ago, in response to my question about whether a certain (foolish and selfish) move would prove jeopardous for me, a channeler assured me that I was in no danger. I trusted the advice and acted on it. It proved one of the worst—and most regretted—decisions of my life. It involved words. It was my fault alone and I will never forgive myself. Looking back, I must acknowledge that my manner of framing the question showed that I already knew, or at least had an instinct for, the answer. The way that we frame ethical or "should I/shouldn't I" questions almost always reflects what we already know or suspect. Never neglect that power in yourself.

*   *   *

Let me offer you my own experience of prayer, recent to this writing. As I lay down these words on a late spring evening in 2021, I have ventured a prayer to Minerva, venerated as the goddess of wisdom in Ancient Rome. Why? I have a cultural affinity for the figure and an attachment to the history of Rome. A series of propitious events led me to identify Minerva as a figure of deific exploration and possibility. I have written a prayer to her and placed it on my home altar. I have made a traditional Roman offering to her of olives and silver. I have also lit two candles to Minerva in silver candlesticks, which I recently purchased at a neighborhood theater's fundraiser. My act of veneration is simple, resonant with tradition, and, I hope, dignified. In return for the granting of my petition, I have vowed to write a book in veneration to Minerva. (You can evaluate my loyalty in the future.)

This example returns me to the question on which this chapter hinges: Does prayer work? Well, here is another verity, written nearly in real time. On a Saturday night in spring 2021, adjacent to the events just described, I bicycled with one of my sons to Grand Central Terminal in Manhattan to see the tripartite statue of Mercury, Minerva, and Hercules above the great station's main entrance. I told him that I was praying to Minerva and that he could hold a petition to her too if he wished. The following day, a Sunday, I took him on a job interview. While he was occupied, I bicycled back to the same statue at Grand Central as well as to another statue of Minerva in Herald Square in Midtown. I made plans to visit still a third statue of the goddess in Brooklyn's sprawling Green-Wood Cemetery. By the time I got back to the interview my son had received an offer on the spot (coupled with another job offer from the day before). But when I arrived home, the strange thing happened. Something so weirdly timed that I can only leave you, the reader, to evaluate it.

Concurrent with writing this book I have been assembling another work. I decided one Sunday evening to write to a friend of mine in Europe—a brilliant artist and publisher who I love and whose work has been a profound influence on me. I asked him if he would be interested in publishing it. But I got only silence. It lasted weeks. I was perplexed, confused, and heartbroken. I had written him with deep feeling and detail and I could not understand the absence of a response. (I briefly reference this episode in chapter one.) Through a strange twist of events on my Minerva Sunday, however, something unexpected occurred.

Another European friend, a magician, had written an article, which I emailed him to praise. I began thinking that the publication where his piece appeared might be right for the work of still another acquaintance. I asked the other friend if he would like an introduction to its editor. He said yes. As I wrote my introduction, I visited Amazon in order to hyperlink my friend's book. While I was there, the retail site recommended a book from my *first* friend in this story—the one from whom I had received no reply. That got my emotions going. I forwarded my original email to my partner and said how perplexed I was by my publisher friend's silence. The instant I hit "send," however, I got a Gmail notice that "one of the items in this chain is spam." I was offered the option to unsend the forwarded message or unflag the spam. I unflagged it, whatever it was. *It was the reply from my friend—written almost a month earlier.* The response for which I eagerly awaited had, for no obvious reason, ended up in a spam folder. All my conflicted emotions were the byproduct of a tech glitch. A simple error. The error was now undone. This turn of events, strange on its own, *squared exactly with the nature of my prayers to Minerva.*

Materialists often note that events we perceive as surprising, synchronous, or highly unlikely are, in actuality, not altogether unusual based on the probability of seemingly outlying events occurring across a vast population. In a 2021 essay about his father's UFO encounter, metaphysical writer Harv Bishop noted:

> Of course, this will raise the often-invoked skeptics' fallback argument when dealing with anomalous phenomena: the law of large numbers. The odds of any particular suburban dad having a spicy food-induced dream about UFOs the same night multiple witnesses see a UFO in the area are small. The odds that it will happen to some dad among the countless dads in the world are higher.

As Harv went on to observe, the "large numbers" argument hits a decided limit. Although actuarial tables tend to accurately measure life events across a populace, statistics alone cannot adequately evaluate the depth, weight, and range of emotional context that an *individual experiences* in connection with an event. Such reactions are relevant and highly subjective. They can be deeply intimate. They are not easily communicated or weighed. This is especially true when emotions run at a pitch.

Ironically, or perhaps inspiringly, professional skeptic Michael Shermer made the same point in an October 2014 column in *Scientific American,* "Anomalous Events That Can Shake One's Skepticism to the Core." Shermer described a mysteriously timed musical "message" from a busted heirloom radio on his wedding day, which evoked the palpable presence of his bride's deceased and longed-for grandfather. The event not only had infinitesimally small odds but, perhaps more importantly, profound personal significance.

"What does this mean?," Shermer asked, continuing:

Had it happened to someone else I might suggest a chance electrical anomaly and the law of large numbers as an explanation—with billions of people having billions of experiences every day, there's bound to be a handful of extremely unlikely events that stand out in their timing and meaning. In any case, such anecdotes do not constitute scientific evidence that the dead survive or that they can communicate with us via electronic equipment.

Yet, he confessed, "I have to admit, it rocked me back on my heels and shook my skepticism to its core as well.

I savored the experience more than the explanation. The emotional interpretations of such anomalous events grant them significance regardless of their causal account."

In January 2014, I wrote in my *One Simple Idea*:

> Statistics are wonderful for measuring odds, but not for measuring the emotional gravity that one attaches to them. It can be argued that emotions are incidental to odds. But not entirely. An event is notable not solely for its odds . . . but for the *quality of the event's meaning* given the expectations and needs of the individual.

The skeptic and I reached the same conclusion. This begs the question of whether the skeptic-seeker divide is due more to polemics than empirical differences.

Needless to say, my emotions ran at such a pitch in the prayer scenario I just described: my friend had dramatically impacted the direction of my career and search; the perception of not hearing from him was emotionally difficult. The rarity of the salving event stands beyond reasonable likelihood when the mix of emotions, history, and timing are factored in. My prayers, it seems, were answered.

One last note. Some events are so unlikely that we would deny their very possibility were it not for the actual incident. For example, the Centers for Disease Control estimate the odds of getting struck by lightning in a given year at 1:500,000. Getting struck twice in a lifetime is 1:9,000,000. Virginia park ranger Roy Sullivan (1912-1983) holds the world record for getting struck *seven different times.* The odds of that are estimated at 1:10,000,000,000, 000,000,000,000,000,000 or 10 to the 28th power. It is a number so large that we almost never use it. If you factor in Roy's survival, the odds are near-incalculable. I note this not to suggest anything supernatural about Roy's life. But I can report that when a producer friend inquired about the episode with a physician who specializes in lightning strikes, the medical professional dismissed her query: "It's just random chance." Well, we do not know that. For one thing, so few people have ever had commensurate experiences (if such a thing can even be posited) that the matter has never been studied. Indeed, were this scenario posed as a "what if?" rather than a medically documented event, it would be considered impossible. But, "Impossible events do not occur," wrote parapsychologist Lawrence LeShan in his 2009 *A New Science of the Paranormal.* The extraordinary exists only after the fact.

*   *   *

Postscript to my prayer experience: On Memorial Day, 2021, I visited a bronze, life-sized statue of Minerva that stands at the highest point in Brooklyn on a hill in Green-Wood Cemetery. The armored goddess of wisdom, her head wearing a helmet capped by a sphinx and her breast-plate engraved with the aegis of her defeated foe Medusa, gazes across New York Harbor to meet the eyeline of the Statue of Liberty to whom Minerva raises her left hand in tribute. The goddess's right hand holds a garland of victory and rests on a stone pillar, where visitors some-times leave small offerings, such as polished stones, keys, and shells. I left a little wooden bowl with the traditional offering of olives. If you visit, you may still find the bowl wedged beneath the goddess's bronze wreath. I tucked a written petition beneath her sandaled feet.

Upon completing my pilgrimage, I biked a few miles away to a waterfront park in Williamsburg, Brooklyn. I walked my bicycle into the park, settled into a bench in a sunny spot, and called artist and friend Josh T. Romero for a Master Mind meeting. After about ninety minutes, I began walking my bike out of the park. As I wheeled the bike into the street and began to mount it, I noticed on the asphalt directly under my feet a card with handwriting that looked like my own. I jarringly realized that it was an index card, cut in half and laminated with clear packing tape, on which I had written my definite chief aim in red marker. The statement was highly personal—and there it was lying face up in the street. It had obviously (and oddly) fallen from my front jeans pocket as I entered the park.

Now, this was a heavily traveled street at the entrance to a popular and packed spot on a sunny Memorial Day. The odds of my dropping and then finding the card in the same spot were unusual. Emotionally (if not, perhaps, statistically), it seemed like the card had "found me." I felt as though I was rediscovering my own destiny. Had a stranger picked up my home-laminated card, that person, depending on outlook, might have seen it as a "sign" of his or her future; or perhaps a provocative art project (someone spreading cards around the city that disclose people's fate); or just some sidewalk debris to be kicked away. But that I, its writer, stumbled upon it—and that its statement comported exactly with what I had just prayed for at Green-Wood Cemetery—struck me as portentous.

* * *

Urgency is distinctly important to prayer. Prayer, in my experience, resists casualness. As further explored in chapter eight, "The Wish Machine," *deliverance often follows despair or near-despair.* These are polarities of life. In order for the aforementioned pendulum swing of events or awareness to reach one vector point it is often, and perhaps lawfully, necessary that it first reach the other. A valuable principle appears in the 1908 Hermetic-based guidebook *The Kybalion*: "rhythm compensates."

Life is unyielding to half-measures. What span or arc does a half-measure traverse other than another half-measure? I have found, however, that the kind of prayer that finally delivers a solution—just like the kind of wish—is felt and expressed with the intensity of an oxygen-deprived being gasping for air. Someone I love was looking for a dramatic turnaround to a depleting problem. She told me that one evening in a deeply personal prayer ritual she *begged*. I was proud of her for making this admission—and of the commitment that it bespoke. I personally witnessed a remarkable and lasting solution reach her within 48 hours. I am currently reviewing these words on a movie set that arose from the contours of her prayer.

Likewise, one Sunday evening—traditionally a depressing hour for me going back to childhood—I reached the conclusion that my continual act of prayer around a major life issue had been too tepid. I wondered:

should I follow suit and *beg*? Yes, I decided. So, I implored; I uttered my need from the deepest, most primal place I could find within my psyche. My prayer was a totalizing act: mental, emotional, physical. I felt and expressed my depth of need and wish for a solution with a rare unity and intensity. I had nothing left in me when I was done. But rather than experience depletion, I felt a sense of resolve. Of completion. I also experienced movement and accompanying morale that I needed in the days that immediately followed.

*   *   *

In this chapter, I have attempted to be vivid and disclosing, but I have not prescribed a precise or by-the-numbers template for prayer. I believe that any structure, approach, or decision regarding prayer belongs to you alone.

For my part, I have prayed on street corners, in cemeteries, in churches, synagogues, and in public buildings, as well as in private. I neither parade nor conceal my dedications. My spirituality is not monochromatic and my search takes many forms, all of them possessed, for me, of inner symmetry. You probably feel the same in your life.

I have elected to be public about my search in my writing. I hope my transparency is useful. There may be periods in which you are more public about your search and other times in which you are more private. I counsel only this: explain yourself to those who ask *but only to a certain point*. People either get it or they do not.

One of the toughest lessons I have learned in life is that no matter how much clarity, earnestness, and good faith you bring to your explanations, you invariably encounter some fraction of people who cannot see past what they really want: which is for you to behave like them. This means obeying them.

When moved or called to explain yourself, do it once. Then be silent. And disobey.

Here is a case in point and a study in human interaction regarding matters of spirituality and belief. It typifies our social-media era, but it belongs to all eras. In the fall of 2020, I joined Greg Salyer, president of the Philosophical Research Society (PRS), in an online forum to celebrate the life and work of esoteric scholar Manly P. Hall and the launch of my book *The Seeker's Guide to the Secret Teachings of All Ages*. In the question-and-answer period that followed, a viewer asked, and Greg faithfully (and rightly) repeated, a direct question. Here is my reply along with one reader's response; I hope you will find the juxtaposition elucidating.

Greg: All right Mitch let's get this over with. You've been waiting for this question: Are you a Satanist?

Mitch: Ah, what a wonderful question. I believe in giving direct answers to direct questions. So, I'm going to give you a very direct answer. And the answer is: yes. However, I also want to give you a very clear answer. And the clear answer is that I have my own individualized conception of what that means. And it's very important to understand that it's impossible to interpret another person's ethical, religious, and spiritual journey through the lens of decisions that other people have made about what a classification is, what a thought system is, what a school is, or, as often happens, through entertainment.

We must be able to define our terms or we wind up defining one another into very narrow corners and spaces. I write about this topic in my book *Uncertain Places* and elsewhere and discuss it in a lecture called "God of the Outsiders," which I delivered in Los Angeles and New York City.*

I believe that we can attempt a very legitimate esoteric reading of a Satanic tradition in the West that understands the Satanic not as a force of evil, violence or malèficence but rather as a force of radical individualism, usurpation, nonconformity, revolutionary change, and the extolling of the individual. I believe that if Adam and Eve had not mythically eaten from the so-called Tree of Knowledge of Good and Evil, humanity itself, and we ourselves, would be incapable of having this exchange right now. They needed to break out of the paradisiacal world in which they were kept and to venture out into a world of friction and difficulty because *friction is the price of creativity*. Without friction we would remain emotional and intellectual children.

Now, I take a radical stance and position and there are people who have come to me and they have said— quite legitimately and fairly—"I groove to everything that you're talking about but must you use the term

---

* Both versions appear on YouTube.

Satan? Do you have to use that language?" They have a point. I am not interested in provoking or pushing buttons or just creating heat. But I also must be frank and straightforward about the nature of my search—or my search is dead. My work and my search are the same.

I often find my way to ideas through a certain persona or a piece of unexamined history, and I began to ask questions about this mythical figure of Satan—although I don't just view the Satanic as metaphorical. I believe that there exist distinct energies with which we can foster relationships, as our ancient ancestors did, and I think that what I am describing represents the most *misunderstood* of those deific presences in Western life. I'm attempting, certainly in my own life and in my writing, to bring a new conception to that idea. So, I hope that adequately answers your question.

Greg: Mitch, when I hear you answer that question voices come into my mind: John Milton, William Blake, and William James.

Mitch: Oh absolutely, without question. Blake and Milton are probably two of my greatest sources of inspiration. There are other, modern sources of inspiration, including Michael Aquino and Anton LaVey. I don't embrace everything that they're about but they, too ... have demonstrated elements of brilliance, which have certainly helped me. But my search is entirely my own.

To this exchange, I have gotten positive replies, sharp questions, and, well, responses like this one on social media:

> I read your article trying to be open because I want to respect other viewpoints than my own. I am spiritual but I am not religious or pious in any way. Having said all that Satanism is so baffling to me. Why not just be an atheist? Isn't it more subversive in a way? Satanism just seems pointless and bombastic. Sorry.

You know this person. You have shared Thanksgiving with him or her. This is the person to whom you say, for example, that you are a socialist, and you get conflated with Pol Pot. Or you say that you are a libertarian, and you get equated with the Sackler family of Oxycontin infamy. Sometimes no matter *how much* you explain you cannot be heard. That reality does not make me cynical. I believe in sharing the facts of my path—to a point. In considering the limits of language and rational analysis, twentieth-century philosopher Ludwig Wittgenstein concluded in his 1922 *Tractatus Logico-Philosophicus*: "Whereof one cannot speak, thereof one must be silent." Throughout this chapter, I have sought to extend as far as I can to the point of silence. That point is reached—further territory must be entered by your own experience. Go and seek.

Chapter Seven

"We Are Mighty"

A pivotal moment in my search occurred one evening when a senior member of a spiritual group I was in made a simple declaration: "There are no shortcuts."

That kind of statement, so commonsensical on its face that there appears nothing to argue over, so quotidian that the person who uttered the words probably would not recall the episode, set me to vow that I would never accept such claims without personal verification. How could either he or I know whether there exist shortcuts or accelerants on the path?

The speaker may have been right. But with the stakes so high—amounting to the nature of one's existence—I would never accept such statements without scrutiny. As a result, the counterclaim, "How do I *know* that's true?" became one of the core and recurring questions of my search. For that, I must thank my interlocuter.

Years later, I have, in fact, discovered one experience that fosters rapid change. I would not exactly call it a shortcut but it is among the most effective, immediate, and dramatic vehicles for attaining a new sense of personal power. It is the experience of an epiphany, which is a moment of stark, even preternatural clarity. Such an experience can form the basis for a revolutionized perspective on reality and self. An epiphany can objectively reconstitute your conduct and abilities, much like what William James called a "conversion experience." In his 1907 essay *The Energies of Men*, James wrote:

> *Conversions*, whether they be political, scientific, philosophic, or religious, form another way in which bound energies are let loose. They unify us, and put a stop to ancient mental interferences. The result is freedom, and often a great enlargement of power. A belief that thus settles upon an individual always acts as a challenge to his will. But, for the particular challenge to operate, he must be the right challengee. In religious conversions we have so fine an adjustment that the idea may be in the mind of the challengee for years before it exerts effects; and why it should do so then is often so far from obvious that the event is taken for a miracle of grace and not a natural occurrence. Whatever it is, it may be a highwater mark of energy, in which "noes," once impossible, are easy, and in which a new range of "yeses" gains the right of way.

Conversions or epiphanies are not always happy in the conventional sense. But they are profoundly meaningful and—if heeded—potentially seismic in terms of self-image, actions, and experience. They reconstitute who you think you are or must be.

A psychologist once told me about the power of epiphanies in the lives of some of his patients. He related a story about an awakening experienced by a woman in a loveless marriage to a ruthless man. She had recently discovered her husband's infidelity and he responded by demanding a divorce. This woman had dedicated herself for years to someone who was now summarily dropping her; what's more, her husband's hardened personality presaged a bitter divorce battle, in which he would fight to leave her with as few resources as possible.

She later told the therapist that as she left his office and began walking through the building's parking lot she experienced, without filter or rehearsed responses, the stark reality of her situation. "I am," she thought, "completely alone in the world. I have absolutely no one to depend on."

Her realization—her epiphany—did not trigger despair. Instead, the experience left her with a surprising feeling of weightlessness, liberty, and possibility.

As she faced the hardcore truth of her situation, she felt not weakness but power. Not fear but agency. She felt liberated from the persistent doubts, anxieties, and conflicting voices that had been running through her head. Her *total embrace of reality* brought with it a dramatically renewed sense of self. She was, for the first time in her marriage, self-possessed.

A New Thought hero of mine, Helen Wilmans (1831–1907), reported a similar episode. Wilmans worked as a newspaper reporter in Chicago in the early 1880s. She was one of the pioneering female reporters of the era. Wilmans covered a labor beat and was adamantly pro-worker. She was a populist reformer. But Wilmans also felt frustrated and limited by politics because she believed that many American workers disregarded the tools, both political and personal, that would deliver them victories.

In a *Chicago Express* article called "Willing Slaves of the Nineteenth Century," Wilmans complained that most workingmen lacked any sense of personal aim, self-betterment, or higher aspiration. Granted the chance, she wrote, they did not want to build a new world for themselves and others; given their druthers they would trade places with their bosses, shake down their neighbors, and keep women one rung beneath them. The problem, Wilmans argued, stemmed less from social forces than from the mental habits of most workers themselves:

> The moment one of you begins to think he ceases to belong to that class to whom this article is addressed. Are you willing to come up to the dignity of manhood by an effort to comprehend the true situation and to arouse within your brain the thought that will meet it? . . . The world calls on all men now for brain. It asks you for thought, that through thought it may develop the finer and as yet unexplored forces of nature.

Whatever the abuses of the ownership class, the real problem, Wilmans told the workingman, is: "You will not think." In her burgeoning New Thought outlook, the reporter felt certain that human liberation could be summoned only by fresh thought and personal action. Laborers needed to realize a "sense of power in themselves."

This instinct emerged from Wilmans' personal experience. She had been fired from jobs, divorced from her farmer husband, left to raise two daughters on her own, and she lived one step ahead of eviction from her Chicago boardinghouse. More than anything, the metaphysical crusader yearned to start her own labor newspaper. She wanted to bring the ideas of mind-power to working people.

One day in 1882, Wilmans asked her editor at the *Chicago Express* if he would invest in her new venture. He dismissed the idea out of hand. In despair Wilmans ran from the newspaper offices and wandered through Chicago's darkening streets on a November afternoon. She had an experience like the one related by the woman in the parking lot. Wilmans thought, *I am completely alone; there is no one on whom I can depend.* But as those ideas sounded in her head, the reporter felt suffused with a strange and even intoxicating sense of confidence.

"I walked those icy streets like a school boy just released from restraint," she wrote in 1899 in *The Conquest of Poverty.* "My years fell from me as completely as if death turned my spirit loose in Paradise." It occurred to her that she was not bound in dependency to another person—she had the power of her mind. That, at least, was her version of the New Thought gospel. Wilmans went on to start a newspaper and later a modest metaphysical publishing empire. Her life was not free from strife. But she did attain her aim and serve as a role model to others yearning to break free.

*   *   *

I have a strange relationship to the material in this chapter. Ostensibly, I am an advocate of positive-mind metaphysics. But I also believe deeply in the experiences—generations apart and yet strikingly similar—of these two figures who embraced the bleeding edge of life. Facing reality, steely eyed and plainly, can produce resolve that a thousand affirmations never will. Never avoid the thorns.

As I write these words, I wrestle with a personal haunting of my own. I find that as far as I have come in my career as a writer, speaker, and media figure, I still experience, as many media figures do, getting blown off by potential backers, employees at book and audio publishers, and producers. People give their word and break it. They leave timely and legitimate emails unanswered. They mishandle projects.

In such situations, there is not much that a person can do. Where is my or your power to reverse such behavior? Classicist Mary Beard observed that Rome's first emperor, Augustus Caesar (63 BC–14 AD), provided a playbook in how to gain and retain power: 1) Generosity: dispense lots of goodies and bounty. 2) Build: create monuments and public works; employ people. 3) Conquest: in Ancient Rome this meant seizing land, people, and resources. Hail Caesar—but, for the rest of us, good luck.

As I sat pondering this situation on a spring day, I realized: unless someone has a specific need or wish (including financially) to be in proximity to me and my work, I lack resources to alter the fecklessness that persists in many precincts of culture and commerce. I cannot understand much less change this behavior. Nor can I necessarily alter it by "picturing" a different outcome. Certain stationary barriers appear in life no matter how great my philosophical idealism. Honestly facing this fact is, I am convinced, critical to its resolution.

The truth of my situation is that nothing other than self-sufficiency will ameliorate this kind of crisis. Nothing. If someone does not perceive value in what you or I do today or may do tomorrow *they must be cut off to the greatest extent possible*. They will never dispense value, help, or collegiality. If, however, someone is sympathetic toward my or your aim, we will find each other as assuredly as the attracting poles of a magnet. In fact, even a serious mishap can be endured when parties are in rapport.

A case in point occurred the day before I wrote these words. I was booked to appear on the podcast of a significant contemporary artist whose work I love. I had the date marked and was looking forward to it. Then something occurred that *almost literally never happens*: I forgot. I was overworked, on the road, stressed out, and eager to spend additional time with my partner at an out-of-town film festival. I would never—never—blow off an engagement. When I realized what I had done—twenty minutes past our start time and stuck in out-of-state traffic!—I was mortified. The artist had even endured two hours of LA's crawling traffic to reach a friend's studio for our recording. I apologized profusely and sincerely. His reaction? He was totally cool about it, as was his studio host; we set a new date and time for several days later. My apologies and embarrassment were wholly earnest. But more striking was his willingness to roll with it. Now, my error—a major one—was due to my being overworked and overextended. But his response was so gracious because there existed *genuine sympathy between us.* Even my mess up could not kill that. Were that same quality of sympathy absent, no amount of diplomacy could manufacture it.

*   *   *

Another true story: just as I sat writing these words in an airport, two distribution offers rolled in for a feature documentary on which I am collaborating. Right after that a no-show audio producer got back to me after almost two weeks of ignored emails. Both developments reflected *immediate* reversals of the kinds of non-responsive behaviors I just noted. In fact, these two episodes were among the very examples I was holding in mind. So, what, if anything, changed? Well, for my part, I faced the fact of my powerlessness and vowed to get along *without* the help of those people, no matter how highly or modestly placed, who would not *earnestly work with me.* Rather than bring hopelessness, acceptance brought a seismic shift. Or seemed to. As elsewhere in this book, I am moved to fairly ask whether happenstance or design is at play. Yet the correlation of attitude to event is stirring. And the feelings involved are deeply affirming. According to philosophical pragmatism, that is testimonial evidence.

I also began to feel that perhaps the third parties themselves were not to blame, or not entirely. Perhaps I am to blame because I have allowed myself to get lulled into a kind of complacency. I have embraced media situations or gigs that may be too easy. Easy gigs attract lazy people. I am the furthest thing from lazy, at least when I am impassioned for a project or prospect. I work incredibly hard. I log long hours and happily. *But if I am bumping against the wrong kinds of people then I am clearly in the wrong kinds of neighborhoods.* Hence, I began wondering if questionable collaborators were just a reflection of the broader scene to which I have willingly succumbed.

Scenes must change. A given situation may be helpful and even liberatory at a certain time and place. But circumstances evolve. I realized, as I encountered this epiphany about withholding my collaboration from unmotivated or mediocre workmates, that I may need to face the prospect of making a greater change—a change that may, for a time, leave me less financially supported. But more capable and right.

In Romantic poet Lord Byron's 1821 play *Cain*—a retelling of the Biblical fratricide from Cain's perspective as a tormented outsider—the title character asks Lucifer: "Are ye happy?" The Dread Emperor replies: "We are mighty." That is the kind of reply I wish for everyone who faces his or her situation in the stark light of epiphanic realism.

The decision is entirely yours. Can you already feel the relief that that prospect holds?

Chapter Eight

The Wish Machine

E arlier I considered the power of a wish. I ask now: Is there such a thing as a wrong wish? A wish that causes suffering and sorrow rather than deliverance? A wish that will, in the long run, deplete and degrade rather than fulfill?

These are difficult subjects because they are fraught with cultural prejudices and a tendency toward recited and untested decisions and insights. And there is an added dimension of complexity. Is my wish another's ruin? Is my joy another's despair? I do not necessarily see those prospects as symmetrical imperatives; but it must be acknowledged that for every "win" there is a commensurate "loss." Even your wish for understanding or truth—if sincere—can remove you from the company of people who desire your closeness. Hence, can there be a truly non-violative wish?

These are critical questions. Because your wishes may very well come true. I warrant the existence of a "wish machine." That term appears in the 1972 Soviet-era science-fiction novel *Roadside Picnic* by brothers Arkady and Boris Strugatsky. It served as the basis for the 1979 movie *Stalker* directed by Andrei Tarkovsky. Both are extraordinary works. The pressures of living in a censorious, officially materialistic society drove these Russian artists to reach some of the finest insights we possess on metaphysical causes and effects, cloaked in the garb of science fiction. Do not fear pressure; its burdens, if not overwhelming or fled from, can produce refinements in thought and output.

On a personal scale, pressure to meet intense deadlines has made me a better writer. Pressure to speak publicly when dealing with unforeseen stresses has improved my presentations. I once received a menacing email just before having to go on camera to speak as part of a CNN documentary. I took a breath and thought: this is where you must be a professional. I delivered an interview that I am proud of. The experience served as a milestone to which I look back whenever I find myself wondering if I can function publicly under pressure.

Back to *Roadside Picnic*. The near-future novel depicts a world in which aliens have visited and just as mysteriously departed. The extraterrestrials occupied and left behind a "Zone" where they discarded advanced technology and inscrutable space junk. Humanity struggles (and mostly fails) to understand these advanced castoffs and tools; the alien devices cause strange, unexpected, and sometimes nightmarish effects. Within the Zone exists a rumored *wish machine*, also called the Golden Sphere. This otherworldly device grants you whatever you want—*and only what you want*. The wish machine reads your psyche.

The book's anti-hero, Redrick Schuhart, or Red, is a *stalker*, one of the pirates who illegally enter the Zone to scavenge alien technology to sell on the black market. A young protégé accompanies Red into the morphing and dangerous landscape of the Zone. Using an outdated map, the treasure hunters make their way across burning ground and other perils to reach the wish machine. Red asks his trainee what he will request if they make it. When the youth starts rattling off idealized responses about universal happiness, Red cuts him off: "Liar, liar . . . Keep in mind, buddy: the Golden Sphere will only grant your innermost wishes, the kind that, if they don't come true, you'd be ready to jump off a bridge!"

Their harrowing journey succeeds. They reach the Golden Sphere. Upon seeing the object, the youth flies into rapture, rushes forward and asks for world happiness. The alien object—which Red observes is "closer to copper, reddish, completely smooth"—immediately annihilates the boy. Was it because, as Red suggested, he lied? Or was it because his wish required his own destruction? Red ponders:

Let us all be healthy, and let them all go to hell. Who's us? Who's them? If I'm happy, Burbridge is unhappy; if Burbridge is happy, Four-Eyes is unhappy; if Raspy is happy, everyone else is unhappy, and Raspy himself is unhappy, except he, the idiot, imagines that he'll be able to wriggle out of it somehow. My Lord, it's a mess, a mess!

Red approaches the Golden Sphere himself to make his wish. Not knowing what to ask, his racing thoughts and conflicts give way to his making the same wish as the dead youth. Did it work? Did it destroy him? Did something else occur? We do not learn. "In reality nothing was ever the way people imagined," one of Red's antagonists muses.

*   *   *

I believe that the wish machine is real. If I did not, I would not be so concerned with the issues raised in this chapter and book. In fact, this chapter is a little like approaching the wish machine: we must do so carefully, at times indirectly, and always with caution.

Life lived in a certain way is the wish machine: we move toward and receive a great deal of what we want, albeit unconsciously in most cases. There exists only the most tenuous bond of memory between wish and event. Deliverance often reaches us, or we it, in a form that is unforeseen or even unrecognized.

Indeed, all the alien technology left behind in *Roadside Picnic* gets compared to rubbish tossed off by road trippers who paused for a picnic. The otherworldly debris produces what seem like miracles—often "cruel miracles" with bizarre consequences and no comprehensible cause-and-effect. This is not unlike the human position regarding religion. We are left with insights, rules, principles, relics, and rituals—but do we possess the means to use them, or do these things remain objects of wonder, confoundment, and, not uncommonly, destruction? This situation is worsened when we reduce vast complexities to homilies like, "there are no accidents" or "everything happens for a reason." To trifle with such ideas, rather than fall to your knees and sustain them as lifelong questions, is to toy with destruction.

A scientist in the book says: "A lab monkey presses a red button and gets a banana, presses a white button and gets an orange, but has no idea how to obtain bananas and oranges without buttons. Nor does it understand the relationship between buttons and oranges and bananas." Isn't this our relationship with most spiritual traditions? We experience fitful results but possess little, if any, sense of the mechanics at work.

Hence, in real life *we must seek clarity of self and wishes.* Self-insight and acknowledgment of your desires—while imperfect and maybe at times out of reach—must be striven for. Because *clarity of effort is the one verifiable lever of the wish machine.* I will shortly provide an example of this—perhaps the most valuable example I know.

Before approaching that point, however, I must note that if we are blind to our real wishes, *the wish machine nonetheless acts upon them.* We often become recipients of our alienated desires. We claim no recognition of the fate we have fostered. This is the frightful bargain life offers us. The price of self-estrangement is that we insist that our wishes lay in one direction but, ineffably and unfailingly, the psyche and emotions move towards what is *truly desired,* which may be in another direction. Self-acknowledgement provides not ease but recognition. And something more.

*   *   *

Before providing the example I referenced, I must ask your patience for a further bit of background. Up to this point in my career—and I hope always—I have made myself available for emails from anyone who wishes to write me. I disapprove of the manner in which many editors, gatekeepers, and media arbiters distance themselves from the public. People are sometimes incredulous that I post my personal email online. "Don't you hear from a lot of crazies?" I get asked. In fact, my openness seems to deter frivolity. I receive very little hate mail. I once did an episode of Coast to Coast AM about my personalized definition of Satanism and, to my surprise, I got almost no vituperative remarks. I do receive a few presumptuous requests or solicitations. But, above all, I really like hearing from readers with pertinent stories, results, thoughtful comments, and sincere questions, usually proffered with respectful brevity. I always reply to such notes or try to.

I heard from one such reader in spring of 2021. He told me that he had selected a major aim in life—but it was grinding him down. I generally applaud someone arriving at a focused and well-honed aim, which, as I have alluded, does more than anything to harness your energies. As with nature so with your psyche: concentration produces power. But this reader explained that he was experiencing serious emotional difficulty in sustaining his aim. Rejections and slow progress were depleting him. "My aim is causing me pain," he wrote. "Should I continue or change course?"

I considered his question carefully. Because it has also been my question. I never respond to such queries in platitudinous ways. Hexagram 36 of the ancient Chinese pictogrammatic oracle the I Ching reads: "Persistence

amounting to madness should be avoided."* Hence, I
will not make persistence into an orthodoxy. To be sus-
tainable, the path of attainment must offer respites—and
occasional victories. It should not function as a protracted
source of doubt and suffering.

Now, like the questioner, I, too, have experienced episodes where I felt that my aim was a failure and I had to
change course. But often within about 24 hours I would
unintentionally rebound from those periods of despair. My
wish would reassert its pull, regardless of my melancholy.
I thought carefully and responded: "An aim deterred or
slow in arriving can feel as though it takes the very life out
of our skin. But I also believe that *some things are the source
of what we are living for.* If your aim feels to you this way,
I urge you to hold onto it. A true aim, one that speaks to
your deepest sense of self, asserts its own need to exist. It
has a rightful claim on us."

He wrote back with thanks, feeling seen and validated.
And I felt seen by his question. That is the nature of an
authentic exchange. Such exchanges belong to our era in
ways that traditional teachers do not. At this moment, we
no longer live in an age of great teachers. I once asked a
philosopher friend why it appears that the great teachers—
the Steiners, the Gurdjieffs, the Krishnamurtis—belonged
to past generations but not to our own. "Today," he replied,
"we have the group." The exchange is what belongs to our
era. That is why I honor directness and transparency on
the path, along with sincere and unconditioned questions
and responses. I revile the opposite: cleverness, ripostes,

---

* I am using John Blofeld's excellent and underappreciated 1968 translation.

sarcasm, and obscurantism. Real questions are our sole resource. Recitation, self-inflation, and orthodoxy squander that resource. Do not come near me with off-the-shelf expressions or fortune-cookie homilies.

Regarding individual purpose and striving, *I believe greater peace is found in failure that results from authentic effort than in philosophies that counsel impersonal distance from aim and realization.* This is part of why I embrace the principle: *Try.* It was the slogan of the original Miracle Club from 1875. This was a small group of seekers that later coalesced into the Theosophical Society.

The urge to try is not a salve for failure or a substitute for success. Like everyone reading this book, I want my wishes actualized. I know of one formula for that. The formula is the wish machine, to which we now return.

*   *   *

I spent several years of my adult life in a circle of seekers dedicated to working with the ideas of philosopher G.I. Gurdjieff. The experience was profound and changing. It remains with me every day. In my estimation, the work brought by Gurdjieff is truth itself. Gurdjieff's philosophy strips away fantasy like nothing I have ever encountered. The circumstances in which the teacher worked and struggled—and the methods he passed down—permit no illusion. For Gurdjieff and his immediate circle, life, death, and survival, particularly in the wake of the Russian Revolution, from which the teacher and a band of followers fled at great personal cost, were palpable presences. Immense effort, both physically and in the direction of inner work, was required of every student. This work continued in varying lines following the teacher's death in 1949. Hence, when Gurdjieff made an observation, it was and remains a statement that must be regarded with stark seriousness. I want to share one such observation.

In his posthumously published autobiographical treatise, *Meetings with Remarkable Men*, Gurdjieff described episodes from when he and some of his followers fled civil war-torn Russia. He called attention to certain of these events in an epilogue, "The Material Question," which addressed the need for money and resources. In the summer of 1922, after a dangerous flight across Eastern Europe and Eurasia, Gurdjieff and his students reached Paris with razor-thin resources. Procuring an old estate to function as living quarters and a school, Gurdjieff used every means and prospect to foster his circle's financial survival.

"The work went well," he wrote, "but the excessive pressure of these months, immediately following eight years of uninterrupted labours, fatigued me to such a point that my health was severely shaken, and despite all my desire and effort I could no longer maintain the same intensity."

Seeking to restore his health through a dramatic change in setting and to fundraise for his nascent institute, Gurdjieff devised a plan to tour America with 46 students. The troupe would put on demonstrations of the sacred dances they practiced, present Gurdjieff's lectures to the public, and offer other expositions. Although intended to attract donors, the ocean voyage and lodgings entailed significant upfront expenses. Last-minute adjustments and unforeseen costs ended up consuming nearly all the teacher's remaining resources.

"To set out on such a long journey with such a number of people," he wrote, "and not have any reserve cash for an emergency was, of course, unthinkable." The trip itself, so meticulously prepped and planned for, was on the brink of collapse. "And then," Gurdjieff wrote, "as has happened to me more than once in critical moments of my life, there occurred an entirely unexpected event."

He continued:

> What occurred was one of those interventions that people who are capable of thinking consciously—in our times and particularly in past epochs—have always considered a sign of the just providence of the Higher Powers. As for me, I would say that it was the law-conformable result of a man's unflinching perseverance in bringing all his manifestations into accordance with the principles he has consciously set himself in life for the attainment of a definite aim.

Any time that I experience a slip in my resolve or feel the gnaw of doubt as to the prospect of my cherished aim, I return to his passage. Here is what occurred.

As Gurdjieff sat in his room pondering his possibilities, his elderly mother entered. She had reached Paris just a few days earlier. His mother was part of the group fleeing Russia, but she and several others got stranded in the Caucasus. "It was only recently that I had succeeded," Gurdjieff wrote, "after a great deal of trouble, in getting them to France." She presented her son with a package, which she told him was a burden from which she desperately wished to be relieved. Gurdjieff opened the package to discover a forgotten brooch of significant value that he had given her back in Eastern Europe as a barter item during their flight. He had long ago assumed it was sold and had never again thought of it. But there it was. At just the moment of financial ruin, they were saved. "I almost jumped up and danced for joy," he wrote.

Untiring and focused perseverance are the wish machine.

These are the metaphysical mechanics life grants you. They actualize a penetratingly felt aim. This is no familiar truth. Look more closely. There is more at work in Gurdjieff's story than the simple facts of effort. Although those in themselves, if grasped, would prove valuable. But there is another dimension. Certainty of outcome—*not necessarily in detail but in circumstance*—result from the mechanics he describes.

Again Gurdjieff: ". . . it was the law-conformable result of a man's unflinching perseverance in bringing all his manifestations into accordance with the principles he has consciously set himself in life for the attainment of a definite aim."

A law, by definition, is repeatable, certain, and constant. But a law is also conditioned by circumstance, just as water assumes different forms according to temperature. We do not always possess perspective on circumstance, which is why metaphysical laws are so difficult to detect in operation and result. (This is another reason I so deeply value Gurdjieff's account.) It is also why we sometimes face insurmountable barriers, often in the form of physicality. But we may be assured that there exists *symmetry of reciprocity.* This is described earlier as the pendulum swing of events. This symmetry receives shape and result from effort, just as friction causes heat. Intensity mirrors intensity. We witness this in specifics only after the fact. But symmetry and outcome prevail in tandem.

*   *   *

The pattern I am describing represents a tough bargain because life seems to respond only to an aim abided with *singular passion*. Singularity is difficult when life inevitably presents you with myriad needs, desires, and demands. Hence, your aim must be exquisitely well selected. One impeccably chosen aim can satisfy, or at least touch by adjacency and relationship, many different bases and needs in life, including the needs of people you love. A right aim can frame the world in which you wish to dwell.

Hence, when approaching the wish machine, you must not be a stranger to yourself. You must be uncompromisingly clear about what you want. *Because you will get it.* Ponder that. Reread Gurdjieff's story. Live with it.

In director Andrei Tarkovsky's screen adaptation of *Roadside Picnic, Stalker,* a scenario plays out that relates to the urgency of self-knowledge. (If you would rather not have a part of the movie disclosed, you can view it and return to this point.) In the movie, the wish machine or Golden Sphere is replaced by an area inside the Zone called the Room. The Room grants the wish of whoever survives the journey through the Zone and manages to enter it. We learn that prior to the events of the film, Porcupine, the onetime mentor to the current stalker, hanged himself after returning from the Room. Porcupine had entered the Zone with his brother, who was killed by its bizarrely shifting landscape. Porcupine, however, made it to the Room. He returned home and in a short time became very rich. Apparently, Porcupine's wish was not for the revival of his dead brother but for wealth. He got it. He was so tormented to come face to face with his true priorities that he killed himself.

This is a danger of the wish machine: receiving your alienated wishes. Never approach the wish machine without impeccable self-scrutiny. Never take its powers and possibilities for granted.

*　　*　　*

What is the risk of echoing accepted virtues versus authentically reckoning with self? I personally encounter an inordinate number of passive-aggressive people within the radically ecumenical culture of therapeutic spirituality called New Age. Now, I love the New Age. It supports me. I believe in its open-ended spiritual model. But in nearly three decades of observation as a publisher, writer, and seeker within the New Age—having collaborated with many of its leading voices, presented at its primary growth centers, and met and shared experiences with its acolytes across different continents—I have observed two disproportionately represented flaws among New Age believers: 1) lack of accountability and 2) unacknowledged anger. These traits engender self-undermining and passive-aggressive behavior.

Many, if not most, people within New Age culture work with "Law of Attraction" style methods—*but often without the authenticity that the Room requires of those who are brave or foolish enough to enter it.* Indeed, New Age culture tends to promote the practice of *reprocessing one's wishes through sanitized filters*: i.e., asking for things or circumstances not because they express a profound and stark personal yearning—"the kind that, if they don't come true, you'd be ready to jump off a bridge!"—but, rather, asking through the filtration of ersatz altruism or thinly realized notions of planetary consciousness.

Many New Age acolytes—and I write this as an acolyte myself—experience a half-in, half-out sense of self and striving; they do not clearly identify their wishes; they excuse their own incomplete or even incompetent conduct through claims of detachment or nonidentification; and, hence, they experience a grossly truncated sense of attainment. This produces cyclical resentment.

Let me offer an example to which you may be able to relate in your own experience. Recent to this writing, my partner and I made plans to visit someone with esoteric interests. We flew across the U.S. to do so. (We also had other plans in the area). All our communication with this person, right up to our designated hour, was courteous, clear, enthusiastic, and steady. I texted him twice on the appointed day to inform him of our travel progress. When we were literally a few minutes away, our host casually told us, in response to my text to doublecheck his address, that our visit was now off. He explained that he had left us each voicemails a few minutes earlier to cancel. Why this literally last-minute shuffle? He thought we were arriving too late. It would have to be rescheduled. He made no mention of this earlier in the day in response to my updates. And, in fact, we were not late. He had the timing wrong. By hours. Rescheduling was no simple matter (and we did not—I expect people to keep their word). We had structured our day for weeks around this visit. We traveled across time zones. We cut short an earlier tour to reach him promptly. Yet he insisted in mellifluous tones that we were at fault—right up until I sent him screenshots of our earlier logistical exchanges. Even then, his concession was to recite platitudes, including "everything happens for a reason." That is misappropriating a spiritual principle as an ethical dodge, a common trait in New Age culture. It reminded me of when a metaphysical magazine broke its financial commitment to me only for its manager to ask that I "have compassion for the accounting department."

This is the type of conduct that results from estrangement from self and wishes: unconscious aggression and poor relational maturity. Now, it is unfair to consider New Agers flakes. That is a stereotype. But, as alluded, traits of unaccountability and misdirected aggression are overly represented within New Age culture. This stems from adopting spiritual airs rather than facing one's rough-hewn self. It invites self-negation.

*   *   *

I wish to add one further note about causative mechanics. Gurdjieff's result arrived when he temporarily desisted from his efforts. When he *stepped back*. His trip to America was intended as both a fundraiser and a change of setting and, hence, a fount of vivifying new impressions. The enormity of Gurdjieff's efforts would, for a time, be redirected and thus renewed. Into this gap flowed the solution.

This is a profoundly difficult lesson for me. I do not step back easily or naturally. I rarely divert myself from necessity, or at least my perception of it. I work unceasingly. Indeed, I am writing these words on an airplane as I embark on my first vacation in nearly a year. I face the challenge of whether I can permit new journeys. And with them new solutions. A solution, to be held, requires a vessel. A vessel requires space. I ask each of us together in reading this chapter, separated as we are by time and geography, to radically apply these efforts and thereafter negotiate a break in life. Create a well-timed interval. Allow new forces to make themselves felt. Let us work on this together.

Chapter Nine

Mantra Magick

I s there a perfect way to structure an affirmation or personal mantra? One that imbues your statement with special potency and potential for deliverance?

I have written elsewhere that when structuring affirmations, I do not believe that you need to concern yourself with questions of past or present tense: the key thing is that your affirmation be starkly honest, emotionally passionate, and self-persuasive. But there is another critical element: a subtle approach to wording that effectively "charges" your mantra with potency and power, whether suggestive, metaphysical, or both.

I am going to supply this element to you very explicitly in this chapter. In so doing, I am also going to risk personal disclosure not because I wish to be inappropriately self-revealing, which I most definitely do not, but because I believe that I must honor the same unfettered honesty I ask of you throughout this book. I do this by providing you with real-life, real-world examples that have worked for me (along with my failures) and that I wish will work for you, too. I can do none of that if I am cagey, withholding, or coy.

Several years ago, I received an email from a stranger, a reader living in Iceland. It was an uninvited and non sequitur note. He told me that he wanted to share with me a mantra or affirmation that had reached him several years earlier and that he believed might be helpful to me. His timing was mysteriously propitious. I receive these types of reader suggestions from time to time, and this one proved notable. I liked his non-intrusive tone. I liked his brevity, which usually connotes solidity. He did not ask me for anything. He intriguingly addressed a personal need. I was going through a divorce and life-transition at the time. I was entering a new existence but was also intent on honoring my old one and the ties within it that deeply mattered to me and continue to. The new must honor the old. Life is whole.

I must be personal with you if I am to be honest. The mantra he shared was: *I have intimate relations with beautiful women*. I acted on his suggestion and used the mantra he supplied. As mentioned, my marriage was ending. However—and note this carefully—*I was not looking to "play the field*," nor did I. I personally believe that human nature is too discursive and stormy for anyone to seek random hookups or multiple partners. That is not a formula for happiness. It is a formula for chaos. I did, however, enter some new relationships, and in a relatively short time found myself in an immensely rewarding long-term relationship, which has continued for about three years as of this writing. In fact, that relationship has resulted, among other things, in the home in which I reside today. I will say it plainly: the mantra worked. Or at least it reflected lived reality.

I asked myself what I could learn from the experience and how or whether it could be repeated using like-structured mantras. I discovered the answer early one morning in June 2021. At that time, I found myself facing a financial crisis. It involved my least favorite subject: health insurance. You can read about the episode in detail in my book *Cosmic Habit Force*, where I explore the power of emotional necessity in solving a problem. For our purposes here, however, I want to talk about how *I detected and applied a formula that made the first mantra work*, or seemed to, and how it fitted my financial needs.

Pondering all this early one morning while in a period of hypnagogia—the suspended state in between sleep and wakefulness—I arrived at the following mantra: *I earn a prosperous income from a loving audience.* I purposefully devised the statement to reflect the construction of the earlier one.

What formula is at play? First comes the wished-for act: not just any simple movement of life but one characterized by *feeling and personal values.* Returning to the first mantra, *intimacy* implies closeness, both emotional and physical. It is not a throwaway or objectified relationship. The second part reflects who is participatory in the act. Life is based in relationships. Again, in the first case, *beautiful* implies a trait that is obviously augmentative to life. I used it as given.

In the second mantra—*I earn a prosperous income from a loving audience*—I harnessed the same formula.

The wished-for quality—*prosperous income*—implies not only fulfillment but also healthful, sound attainment. It has personal value attached. The second part reflects my relational partner: *a loving audience.* This connotes not only sustainability but also symbiosis. The term further reflects the deep mutual integrity and respect that characterizes the relationship.

So, to restate the formula:

1. Name and characterize the *wished-for thing* or trait. State the value or quality implicit in it, e.g., happy, intimate, prosperous, healthy, and so on.

2. Name and characterize the *relationship* that supplies or completes the wished-for thing, also in a way that clarifies the dynamic of the relationship, e.g., loving, beautiful, wise, helpful, and so on.

The key ingredients are *the healthful thing or trait desired* and the *constructive relationship that fulfills it.*

As alluded, you must be starkly honest about what you want, as I have been in sharing these mantras. There can be no hiding, perfumery, or subterfuge. The emotional tone and content of your statement must be uncompromisingly real. You have the added benefit of doing all this in private, so I hope you will feel no inhibition, nor resent the lack of inhibition that purposefully characterizes my examples, which I offer in hope of assisting your progress.

* * *

Let me provide a further example that I used as part of an act of sigil magick in early 2020 shortly before the Covid lockdown. I recited and rendered into a sigil: *I have a beautiful new home nearby my work.** I later had to smile to myself when I realized that shortly after employing the mantra, I contracted Covid—and worked from home. The events entailed rendering my apartment into a tidy, pleasantly apportioned, and comfortable living-working space. Lesson: beware of unexpected fulfillment! But something more occurred. In November of that same year, I moved into the place from which I am now writing these words: the second floor of a beautiful historic house with a roof deck in Greenpoint, Brooklyn—an apartment that is outfitted with a small home studio from which I deliver lectures and podcasts, and a comfortable abode where I write for hours at a stretch, as I am doing now. It is the very home that I referenced earlier. The thing—*the beautiful new home*—and the relationship—*an environment that abets my work*—were united in desirability, action, and values. In short, my mantra came true. Or at least formed distinct congruency with reality.

*   *   *

The figure who most popularized the use of affirmations or mantras in the modern era was French mind theorist Emile Coué (1857–1926), of whom I am a great admirer. Coué's formula was to whisper to yourself twenty times

---

* You can read about this process and sigil magick in general in *The Miracle Habits*.

just before falling asleep and another twenty just upon waking—i.e., in the hypnagogic state—*Day by day, in every way, I am getting better and better.*

Critics mocked his formula's singsong simplicity; but they failed to notice something that brought Coué considerable validation decades after his death: the mind-explorer specifically prescribed using the mantra during the highly suggestible—but not yet clinically identified—state of hypnagogia, in which, again, you hover between wakefulness and sleep. You naturally enter this state twice a day. It is a period during which conscious reality and dream states intermingle and your rational defenses are lowered. Hence, you are better able to engage in self-suggestion—or what Coué considered self-hypnosis—without the rejection of the rational mind. Coué personally attached no metaphysical significance to his methods. He believed that autosuggestion, or self-hypnosis, simply reprogrammed your psyche to pursue its desired ends confidently and aptly. That may well be part of the equation.

Yet I believe there is a further element to "mantra magick" whereby we, always and at all times, engage in acts of *selection*, which is often, and I believe unsatisfyingly, called manifestation. As alluded earlier, our sensory faculties are tools of measurement. Just as tools of measurement in the particle lab "select" what will appear and when—raising questions of infinite, coexistent outcomes and the illusion of linear time—so are you enacting this process through your *emotional and intellectual perspective.* That, at least, is my theory. And I believe it falls to every generation to venture, however nascently, a delivery system behind metaphysical hypotheses.

Another way to measure actuality is through correlation. This is the basis of philosophical pragmatism, which honors, rather than dismisses, individual testimony. Across time and through meta-analyses, individual testimony forms a record. In fact, we use this approach all the time, such as in measuring degrees of pain or happiness in clinical settings. We rely upon testimony to determine the efficacy of psychopharmacological drugs, which are highly individualized.

Testimony is a keynote of pragmatism. And I defend its pertinence in evaluating metaphysics. So did my philosophical hero William James (1842–1910), whose effort at constructively critiquing New Thought has been neglected since his death. I am attempting to revive that effort. I invite you to join me through our shared practice.

Let me return to my universal mantra and that of the original Miracle Club: *Try.*

Chapter Ten

Determination

Isometimes do Tarot spreads for myself, friends, and loved ones. I find Tarot an occasionally confounding, occasionally revealing tool—and I use it mostly in private. Before describing what I discovered on a particular day, and how it relates to the mind's causative abilities, let me first ask about this method as I have about others in this book: *Why should it work at all?*

As both a student of Tarot's history and a reader of the cards, this question matters to me on more than metaphysical terms. It is ethically important. Whenever I read the cards for myself or someone close to me—my method is a three-card spread in which I seek out a narrative or storyline—I want to be certain that I am doing more than shaking a Magic-8 Ball or flipping a coin. But am I?

In terms of experience, I believe that *something more* than chance or a Rorschach interpretation is occurring. On Independence Day of 2018, I offered free readings to social-media followers. I was celebrating the release of a mini documentary on Tarot in which I had participated.

The response was far greater than I expected. I ended up doing hundreds of readings over a 72-hour period.

Anecdotal though they were, the responses that came back to me were remarkable. A woman who asked about her career path got cards symbolizing justice; she had already enrolled in a police academy. Another who wanted to know where to relocate got cards with two rivers; she had been considering Two Rivers, Wisconsin. Lots of replies were less specific but no less penetrating, including a reading I did for myself that forecast multiple benefits from a project I was uncertain about taking on, but which has since brought me a wide array of opportunities. If there were lots of countervailing or unremarkable readings—and there must have been some—they were not brought to my attention.

For a while thereafter, I started charging modest fees for my readings ($20) and then let my prices inch up. But I often found that when someone wrote me in the depth of need, I could not charge that person. I decided to limit monetized readings to special occasions, such as fundraisers or events for schools like the Philosophical Research Society (PRS) in Los Angeles. At the start of the Covid lockdown in 2020, I offered free readings via email for healthcare workers. As of this writing, I have discontinued all public or commercial readings. I cannot say exactly why. I get lots of requests. If I did not believe in the validity of the readings, I would not do them for myself or intimates. But I suppose I feel that insight-by-the-hour works unevenly and at this stage I do not feel right attaching a fee or a stranger's hopes to such an approach.

Yet the question of why, how, or *whether* a reading is accurate remains important to me. A story is told in the Talmudic book *Pirkei Avos*, or *Ethics of the Fathers*, of a student who encounters a skull floating on dank waters. "How did you get here?" the student asks the skull. "I drowned others with my words," the skull replies, "until my words returned to drown me." I do not want to be that skull.

Based on personal conviction and experience, I have a theory of why Tarot readings can provide mature insight and even foresight. My theory dovetails with an observation made by some of Carl Jung's students. The psychologist and his immediate circle worked with the ancient Chinese oracle the I Ching or "Book of Changes." Like Tarot, the I Ching, when asked a question, "responds" with a parabolic story rendered in pictograms, in this case two out of 64 hexagrams selected by coin tosses or, in the more rigorous traditional practice, by sorting among 50 stalks or sticks. Some observers, including sinologists John Blofeld and Richard Wilhelm, have related the feeling that the I Ching evinces a kind a personality and even humor. A few of Jung's closest students ventured the theory that a pictorial representation, such as an image, symbolic rendering, or sketch, captures a moment in time—but more than just a linear moment. A pictogrammatic image may capture, for a fleeting interval, a multi-dimensional impression of past, present, and future; hence, an I Ching pattern or a Tarot spread might function as a kind of layered photograph or cartoon strip conveying all that is occurring at a given moment, unbound by traditional perceptions of time.

Such an image is not flawless or immune to change, so the theory goes; but it is a reasonable iteration of what is occurring beyond the linear boundaries in which we think. Again: why should that be?

One of the things we have considered is that linearity is an illusion, albeit a necessary one for five-sensory beings to navigate life. Most of the time we gather information through ordinary instruments of sensory measurement—sight, smell, touch, taste, sound—and innately conclude that we know what is going on. Yet quantum theorists, using much finer instruments of measurement, reveal to us a particle world in which infinitesimally small objects occupy states of superposition, or limitless possibilities and potentialities, which become localized only when a sentient observer takes a measurement. Likewise, serious researchers of psychical abilities have produced vast and replicable statistical records of individuals acquiring information in anomalous ways—gleaning images, coordinates, or symbols from a near-infinitude of possibilities without limitation by time, order, or distance, as is extensively explored in chapter twelve. Furthermore, models and observations of speed, light, distance, and gravity have demonstrated—and in some cases proven—that time itself is relative; time necessarily bends, for example, based on speed or extreme gravity. Hence, it is no casual statement to say that linearity *is not a real thing*. That is where Tarot reenters.

If a Tarot spread can be seen as a *measurement*—and in terms of perception, what else is it?—then it follows that its pattern of images may "freeze" or timestamp an event from among a near-infinite range of possibilities.

This localization may be affected by the attitudes and emotions of the card reader, which is why a reader's sensitivities, outlook, ethics, and prejudices matter. (Some are said to possess a "gift" for reading the cards, which may suggest rapport with certain querents.) These localized possibilities may be unbounded by conventional conceptions of time; they can also shift or change based on intervening intentions or forces. But they are, I surmise, a reasonable "weather report" of what is going on beyond our linear thought system and, hence, what is probable in experience.

Tarot is psychologically penetrating because its imagery consists of archetypes that are recognizable and emotionally meaningful to people from probably every culture and time. Death, the Magician, the Emperor, the Wheel of Fortune, Judgement, the Lovers, and so on, form a visual code that proves evocative to nearly every psyche. When we use Tarot, we draw upon a universal language of thought pictures. I should, of course, note that I am specifically referring to the images found in the major trumps of the Florentine and Marseilles decks of the early Renaissance, built upon earlier Hermetic influences and re-envisioned with piercing brilliance by artist Pamela Coleman Smith (1878–1951) in the early twentieth century in the so-called Rider Waite-Smith deck (Rider was the original publisher). I personally use the deck that Smith illustrated and designed with Brooklyn-born British occultist Arthur Edward Waite (1857–1942). I find the Waite-Smith deck not only the ur-text of contemporary Tarot, but a psychologically vivid and intriguing sourcebook on its own.

I believe that Tarot and I Ching possess a shared capacity to tell a story of human relations through a primeval code of archetypal imagery. If approached maturely, the readings that these devices produce are not, in my view, playthings or random hits. They are, I believe, perceptual and extra-linear measurements of the individual story at a given moment.

At one such moment while working on this book, I found myself focused on the future of my career. I used to tell people who asked me for readings never to feel embarrassed, as some were, to inquire about career or romance, which, in one way or another, occupied about 90 percent of requests. (The remainder were health and the direction of one's search.) Life is largely work and relationships. Why turn away from that? Hence, I took out my deck and asked: *What lies before me in the months ahead regarding my work?*

As is my standard practice, I shuffled the deck with this question in mind and spread out the cards face down in a semi-circle. I then selected three cards, laying them face down from left to right. In the same order, I flipped them over. If I encounter a reversed card, I turn it right-side up. My method does not use reversed cards, which I consider a modern artifice and a needless source of anxiety. The 78 cards of Tarot are sufficiently broad in symbolism and vast in potential combinations to convey whatever meaning may be at hand.*

---

* I learned the three-card method, as well as the dispensing of reversals, from artist Robert M. Place. Place's book *The Tarot* (2005) is an invaluable resource; it combines rigorous historicism with respect for the mystical allegory of the cards.

In flipping over the three cards, I received what I consider a lesson in mental causation and determination. Now, the spread I received might be considered unsettling. It was this:

I interpreted this spread as what I call "wings"—when the cards on the left and right reflect and reinforce the card in the center.

The center card, as you can see in the spread, is the Two of Swords, depicting a blindfolded figure of justice holding aloft crossed swords. The figure is in a state of suspended judgment; she is pondering a decision. She cannot hold up the swords indefinitely. Indeed, the figure is seated against a kind of backdrop or curtain of scenery, which seems to fall to the floor of a stage. The artist Smith's framing suggests that the figure is a player or actor; Smith uses this device in several cards. Hence, the scene is temporal. It is impermanent. Judgment is imminently due.

On the right-hand side appears the foreboding Three of Swords in which three swords pierce a heart aloft in

stormy, gray skies. The image suggests sorrow, disappointment, and dashed hopes. It is, of course, an unnerving card.

On the left-hand side, however, appears what is considered one of the noblest and most portentous cards in
the deck: The Chariot. Filled with alchemical and mythical imagery, The Chariot, taken as a whole, suggests
regality, nobility, spirit emergent from matter, marrying
of opposites, appointment, position, and authority. For
some interpreters, the card exoterically conveys material
gain and travel in wealth and luxury.

This spread is, in a sense, a study in polarities, with
the arbiter of judgment or justice perched in the middle.
At first, I interpreted the reading as an intermingling of
success and disappointment. But as I looked further, I
saw something very different. The spread is a lesson of *the
ascendancy of that which the psyche focuses on*. In a sense, this
three-card placement illustrates the premise of this book.

The central figure is blindfolded—she is compelled
to look within. In addition to her blindfold, the cres-
cent moon rises behind her signifying night. The figure
relies not on sensory experience or outer perception but
on inner principle. She is truly impartial. But she cannot
remain suspended in her state; she must reach a determination. Her decision lies between the nobility of the
charioteer and the disappointment of the pierced heart.
She sees neither. Each are *states*. That which she selects
rules the reading. And the reader's experience.

In encountering this triptych, I realized that I con-
fronted the question of just *how seriously* I take my own
mind-causation thesis. Am I *determined* to follow the
methods that I espouse in this book?

I came to see this spread as a *goad toward principle.* Yes, I experience disappointments. I also experience victories. But the unfolding of my work in the months ahead, I realized, *would reflect and emerge from the extent to which my determined perspective rested on the nature of either the charioteer or the pierced heart.* I was challenged to perform an act of selection. Neither polarized card *is*: the figure in the center—blind to sensation and faithful to principle—measures and thus actualizes.

Now, let's say that I am wrong about Tarot. Let's assume that the metaphysical dimensions I describe in this chapter are chimerical. My point still stands. Unless you are willing to believe in the possibility of your greatest attainment, no attainment is possible. You will never venture the risks and sacrifices involved. Self-belief is no guarantee; but it is a prerequisite to all meaningful effort. Hence, believing that which is in line with your greatest good is the core determinant of whether that good has a fighting chance. At the very least, your effort and exertion depend upon it.

Now choose.

Chapter Eleven

Optimism of the Will:
Mind Power as a Philosophy of Life

In spring of 2018, I participated in a live, online chat with listeners of the late-night radio talk show Coast to Coast AM. At the top of the chat, I received a thoughtful and detailed question from a participant named Matt C. He asked me to respond to the critique that social thinker Christopher Lasch (1932–1994) had made of New Age and alternative spirituality, which Lasch saw as mired in narcissism.

Before his untimely death from cancer at age 61, Lasch wrote penetratingly of the increasing segmentation of American society; the distance of social, economic, and cultural elites from the needs of the overall public; and the increasingly maladapted forms by which we seek personal gratification.

As Matt C. described it, Lasch regarded "New Age, Gnostic, and Occult movements as essentially resulting from primary narcissism," in which starry-eyed followers seek to elude death and personal limitation by erasing boundaries and melting into a numinous whole with the universe. The other form of narcissism that defines New Age and alternative spiritual movements, in the listener's summation, is "destructive secondary narcissism, which we associate with egomania and an attempt to restore a sense of lost omnipotence." This occurs when the go-getter personality perceives himself as the center of the universe, possessed of boundless power and entitlement.

In a 1990 afterword to his 1979 classic *The Culture of Narcissism,* Lasch further wrote that New Age revives ancient forms of Gnostic spirituality, stipulating that both modes of practice, with greater sympathy to the poetic pathos of Gnosticism, rely upon infantile fantasies. "The New Age movement," Lasch wrote, "has revived Gnostic theology in a form considerably adulterated by other influences and mixed up with imagery derived from science fiction—flying saucers, extraterrestrial intervention in human history, escape from the earth to a new home in space . . . The New Age movement is to Gnosticism what fundamentalism is to Christianity."

I responded that while I have tremendous respect for Lasch, I believed that he and many academic critics "lacked familiarity with New Age material and its distant antecedents." As I saw it, Lasch "was uncharacteristically under-prepared to critique this aspect of our culture. What

Lasch failed to grasp is that New Age, rather than being steeped in narcissism, is actually a re-sounding of ancient Gnostic themes. It is a varied search for understanding." (Lasch and I both compared New Age with Gnosticism— but with different estimates of the latter's value.*) I defended New Age "simply as a radically ecumenical culture of therapeutic spirituality. It shares the attitude of radical search with ancient Gnosticism." I stand by those remarks. But, looking back, I do not feel that my reply adequately encompassed the depth of Lasch's critique.

If the mind-power thesis as I have presented it in this book is roughly correct, then the issues framed by the Coast listener place the practitioner in front of a daunting question: *What is mind power for*? Is it just a metaphysical ego trip? Or a mode of escapism?

To address this argument, let us assume, as I do, that the mind's causative properties are, too some degree, authentic—something Lasch would have disputed; he probably would have viewed such an outlook as a delusive diversion in the direction of either primary narcissism (i.e., melting into the numinous) or secondary narcissism (i.e., egomania). But I abide by the viewpoint argued in this book—and claim it as my privilege: we all live by assumptions, whether spiritual, materialistic, or some variety. Traditionally, our only empiricism on the path is conduct and experience. I cannot prove or disprove the functionality of my or another's private philosophy beyond the measure of resultant behavior and credible

---

* See my "The New Age and Gnosticism: Terms of Commonality," *Gnosis: Journal of Gnostic Studies*, Volume 4: Issue 2, 2019, Pp. 191–215, also reprinted in *Uncertain Places*.

testimony. I augment that approach with corresponding insights from the sciences, as I bring to bear in this and the following chapter.

*   *   *

If the individual is indicted by a drive to rejoin an idealized numinous state and thus escape the frictions, uncertainties, and imminent end of life—which he or she may seek by erasure of boundaries and assumption of "oneness" with a deity or supernatural forces—or another individual seeks security by an equally childish quest for self-inflation and rejection of obstacles to wish fulfillment and gratification, then such a person must stand in judgment before the question of the purpose and significance of *metaphysics of any kind*—and particularly the type to which I prescribe, which emphasize attainment. In that vein, Lasch would detect in me, and in my prescription, the malady of secondary narcissism: inflation of self.

I referred to attainment. Someone once told me that he did not know what I meant by attainment. At this, I can only smile. If a smoke detector went off at 4 a.m. and someone yelled: *"we have to get out of here!"* no one would ask, "what do you mean?" *We know.* The form that attainment takes is immediately and privately felt by, and distinctive to, every individual. But is the wish to create, produce, earn, generate, or live in a certain way—in short, *is ambition*, even of an ethically developed variety—a *worthy end* of the spiritual search?

I have wrestled with this question for many years. I have come to a perspective on it. At this stage of my search, I have ceased to distinguish between what are considered eternal and temporal values. I believe that any such division is artificial and gets inured in us by the force of familiarity.

Much of Eastern and Western religious thought tells us that we live in a hierarchical cosmos, and things that are essential, eternal, sacred, and everlasting belong to the "greater you," to a higher degree of existence toward which you progress as you shed worldly attachments and illusions, sometimes broadly called *maya* or *samsara*, and come to realize that attachments foster suffering. I believe that this idea, so foundational and familiar, does not suit the life and search of the contemporary seeker. I think it warrants reexamination.

In my observation, we have fallen into a rote and recitative division in which we think in terms of attachment and nonattachment, identification and nonidentification, personality and essence, ego and true self, temporal and eternal. I do not know how you would determine the lines of demarcation among those posited opposites.

A friend used to joke that if you demonstrate some behavior and like it, you say it must come from essence; if you demonstrate something and dislike it, it must come from personality. How would we distinguish where personality ends or blends into essence or where a more temporal desire gives way to a more eternal desire? And how would I evaluate what is urgent in another's life?

At this point in my search, I have come to believe that *the essential purpose of life is self-expression*. Self-expression can take any number of forms that are intimate and necessary to the individual. This is not the same as consumption. Consumption of a gross variety aims to salve a lack of self-expression.

I am opposed to nothing other than barriers being thrown up between the seeker and his or her sense of self-expression. The only thing that I stand against, the only moral code I employ on the path, is that I would never intentionally do anything to block or deter another person from striving for the same human potential that I wish for myself.

Even in our age of decentered and discursive information, we imbibe too many homiletic ideas about what constitutes the search, what reflects progress on the path, and how one would evaluate that progress. As alluded, I believe that the evaluation of the success—a term of which we should be unafraid—of a philosophy, therapy, religious or spiritual viewpoint is *the conduct and experience of the seeker.* This includes the capacity to enter into and sustain satisfying relationships, find one's way in the material world in some manner that is reasonably self-sustaining, and, above all, foster capacity and outlets for self-expression.

In Scripture, we read that the creator fashioned the individual in its own image. In the late-ancient Hermetic manuscript called *The Emerald Tablet,* a similar note appears in the principle you have heard me use before: "as above, so below." If we take either of these notions seriously, if these ideas actually mean something to us—and they are at the heart of the Abrahamic and Hermetic religious systems—they must mean that you the individual are capable of creating within your own sphere, as you were created.

Created from what? Hermeticism teaches that all of existence emanates from an infinite presence from which nothing can be added or subtracted; this original substance has no proportion; it cannot be measured, limited, or contained within concepts of time, space, or dimension. The one thing that we consensually understand as fitting that definition is mind.

As noted earlier, the Hermeticists used the Greek term *Nous* to describe an Overmind that they saw as the source of all creation. These Greek-Egyptian thinkers believed that each individual emanates through concentric spheres of creation from this higher mind.* As a being born of mind, the individual is naturally endowed with corresponding creative abilities within the physical framework in which he or she dwells. But this schema also holds that we are *limited* by the laws and forces of our cosmic framework. "Ye are gods," the Psalmist says, "but ye shall die as princes."

Observation dictates that we live under immensely diffuse laws and forces—of which I believe the law mental causation is one. From what I have written up to this point, it could be inferred that thought is the ultimate arbiter of experience. So much within our world, emergent from both the sciences and religious tradition, suggests this. In referencing *a law of mental causation*, I must add that a law is, by definition, ever operative. This does not mean, however, that it is *experienced uniformly.* H_2O is always water, but water can, of course, be vapor, liquid, or solid depend-

---

* According to Hermetic literature, the supreme mind or *Nous*, uses as its vehicle a threefold process consisting of: 1) subordinate mind (demiurgos-nous); 2) word (logos); and 3) spirit (anthropos).

ing upon temperature. Gravity is constant—it is mass attracted to itself—but you experience gravity differently on the moon than on earth or Jupiter or in the vacuum of space, where gravity seems absent but is still felt because objects are drawn in contact. The law of mental causation may work similarly: it is constant but myriad forces mitigate your experience, sometimes deterring its apparent function. Hence, and contrary to Lasch's suggestion, we do not categorically flee from limits when experimenting with the mind-power thesis.

At the same time, we do witness extraordinary congruencies between events and thought or spiritual appeal, some of which I described in the chapter on prayer. Is there even a difference between thought and spiritual appeal? The sensitized mind may be what we colloquially call spirit. We know from academic ESP studies that the mind evinces extra-physical qualities.* (I explore the ESP thesis in the following chapter.) Extra-physicality is my basic definition of spirituality. As such, mind and spirit may be part of the same scale. Let me share a personal experience, which touches on that prospect.

Several years ago, I was part of a very demanding esoteric order. Many people in the group were intellectually refined and the rigor of the search was deeply felt. Physical demands were placed on us. Seekers could be pushed to their limits. I can assure you that nothing does more, or works more quickly, to skewer fantasies about your-

---

* E.g., a meta-analysis of psychical research data appeared in the flagship journal of the American Psychological Association: "The Experimental Evidence for Parapsychological Phenomena: A Review" by Etzel Cardeña, *American Psychologist*, 2018, Vol. 73, No. 5, 663–677.

self than being awakened at an inconvenient hour in an unfamiliar or physically uncomfortable place to perform some difficult task—you discover your limits quickly. People who are accustomed to succeeding in familiar or comfortable settings, who are considered "wise owls" in their domestic realms, or who see themselves as spiritually advanced, get levelled on a very different scale.

One winter, we were planning a camping trip near the New York-Pennsylvania border. If you have ever gone winter camping in the northeastern United States, you know it can be tough going. I once prevailed upon a friend to join me on a recreational winter camping trip and he adamantly refused. Why? I asked. "Because the best you can possibly hope for is to have a terrible time," he said. My friend was, of course, right; we spent the excursion basically trying to stay alive. But this group trip was planned with a sense of purpose. We were gathering in the woods to join together in the search.

My teacher gave me a particular task in preparation. He mixed in a little humor with it, but it was nonetheless a veritable and meaningful effort. He said that the women in the group were going to sleep in tents in the freezing nights. The men were staying in a cold-water cabin—basically a large, uninsulated shack, which was little better. My teacher said that if the female campers had to get up at night to relieve themselves, in order that they would not have to venture into the icy woods, I was to go out and buy buckets for their tents to serve as chamber pots. But these buckets, he said with a glint in his eye, had to be of a particular type. They had to be pink and heart shaped. If, after really trying, I could find no pink, heart-shaped buckets, it would be acceptable for me to buy red, heart-shaped ones. And if I really found myself out of options, I could finally buy red buckets of a standard shape.

This was before digital commerce exploded, so the search for an unusual item required phone calls and foot visits. I lived on the eastside of Manhattan and I embarked on a search across New York's boroughs for pink, heart-shaped buckets. I did not want to disappoint my teacher and I felt that the task was important on several levels. I put everything into it. I called and visited bed-bath stores, hardware stores, home-good stores, and contractor stores, crossing myriad places off my growing list. I got nowhere. I could not find pink, heart-shaped buckets. So, I decided to switch to Plan B and look for red buckets, first heart shaped and, if that proved futile, of a standard shape. That did not seem too difficult.

But, oddly enough, here I was in New York City—one of the commercial hubs of the world—and I could not find red buckets of either type. Again, I called and visited hardware stores, paint stores, you name it. Nothing. Early one evening, out on a household errand, I told myself, "Well, it's time to call my teacher and admit that I failed. I've searched everywhere for pink, heart-shaped buckets. I searched for red, heart-shaped buckets, and then just regular red, circular buckets—but came up empty." Something told me to wait a bit longer. Do not call him yet.

As this was running through my head, I was standing outside of a little around-the-corner neighborhood grocery store, someplace you run to pick up eggs or milk. I entered the store and headed toward the back to the cold-foods section. When I reached the rear of the store, right there stood a gleaming, brand-new pile of *pink, heart-shaped buckets.* In near-disbelief, I grabbed a stock boy and asked, "What color are those buckets?" He said, "Pink." I asked, "And they're heart-shaped?" Regarding me somewhat strangely he agreed and volunteered, "They just came in today."

I was astonished not only because the odds and circumstances of finding my hallowed item right then and there seemed infinitesimal—this is so even if you use the "law of large numbers," which dictates that across a large population weird things must happen to *someone*—but there was an additional factor. This is something that I referenced in the chapter on prayer. It is critical to recall that even when dealing with actuarial tables, large numbers, and statistical probabilities, there is one thing that statistics cannot really get at: the emotional stakes and personal meaning of an experience. The individual is invested with a certain *something* in relation to the thing encountered—whether a yearned-for relationship, job offering, home listing, crisis averted, stranger who helps, friend who has been long out-of-touch, and so on. The emotional stakes and private meaning of a situation can heighten its rarity and pertinence beyond any measure of chance. That is what I experienced in this situation. It exemplified for me an ineffable truth: there is something lawful about mental exertion.

*   *   *

To focus on just one aspect of the mind-causation thesis, it seems to me that the trigger of conveyance behind thought and circumstance is the uniqueness, dedication and totality of an individual's focus, mental and otherwise. Why should this be? In Hermetic philosophy, all actions, cycles, and events represent a kind of rhythmical swing. This reflects the principle "as above, so below," which I see as a natural over-law. A pendulous, rhythmical swing *necessitates a mirroring swing*. Switching for a moment to standard mechanics, Isaac Newton made the observation, which has been validated in both macro and particle physics, that objects separated over vast distances exert precise mirroring effects over one another, for which we have been unable to fully account. String theory is among the theses developed to explain this mirror effect. Within the schema of string theory, all of reality, from the particulate to the universal, is joined by networks of interwoven strings, providing unseen and extra-dimensional antecedents for observed events, including those that we call chance.

In terms of human endeavor—and I speak somewhat metaphorically, but what else is metaphor than a concept of actuality?—when we dedicate ourselves to an ideal, and we bring totality of effort—mental, emotional, and physical—to concentrate on that point, we set in motion a rhythmical swing. There must be a corresponding motion. That motion moves along the arc of your focus, provided there is no overwhelming counter movement based on another event, action, or physical barrier within your framework.

Psychologically, I am describing the mechanics of the "wish machine," captured in G.I. Gurdjieff's earlier statement as "the law-conformable result of a man's unflinching perseverance in bringing all his manifestations into accordance with the principles he has consciously set himself in life for the attainment of a definite aim."

Is this more than supposition? Is it just a pretty way of describing persistence? To consider that, follow me briefly down a different path. As noted, it strikes me that our senses are nothing more than organic instruments of measurement. If we want to get down to definitions that even a philosophical materialist could love, what else are sight, smell, touch, taste, and so on, than instruments of measurement, which transfer data to your central nervous system or psyche?

As noted, researchers in particle physics have amassed indelible evidence over the course of more than ninety years that a subatomic particle exists in what is called a wave state or a state of superposition: the particle appears in an infinite number of places simultaneously and is not localized, or actual, until a sentient observer decides to take a measurement, or a technical device, such as a photometer, periodically takes one.

There exists debate over whether a device represents a method of measurement distinct from an observer, as well as whether the "collapse" from wave to particle results from an observer's individual psyche or "transpersonal mind behaving according to natural laws," as observed by Bernardo Kastrup, Henry P. Stapp, and Menas C. Kafatos in a May 29, 2018, *Scientific American* article "Coming to Grips with the Implications of Quantum Mechanics." This *transpersonal mind*, the writers continue, "comprises but far transcends any individual psyche," a description similar to the Hermetic concept of *Nous*. The authors compellingly argue that even if a device is used for mea-surement—and thus localization—perception and intent, either of the individual, the meta-mind, or both, remains the determining force.

No one challenges quantum mechanics data. It is uncontroversial. Only its implications are. I invite intrepid readers to look up the aforementioned *Scientific American* article: they will find, I aver, that my descriptions of quantum theory are, if anything, conservative. We are, in fact, witnessing a kind of reality selection in the quantum lab, not strictly pertaining to particle behavior but to the nature of observation and creation—or, again, selection—from among infinite, coexisting realities. A decision to measure or not measure sets in motion innumerable possibilities. This is the "many worlds" interpretation of quantum physics. A law, as noted, must be constant. Not necessarily transferable to every situation and not liber-ated from mitigating or surrounding circumstances, but not isolated in data or effects.

The logical conclusion to which quantum mechanics has brought us in the early twenty-first century is that consciousness, or the psyche, cannot be extracted from physics and material existence. All is entangled or *whole*. Hence, if our senses function as devices of measurement, it nudges us in the direction of self-selection. I sometimes encounter critics lampooning or disparaging the New Age perspective on quantum physics—and it must be acknowl-edged that excesses and cherry-picking *do* exist. But when those observers who are actually in the know venture their own description, it often sounds a lot like the New Age interpretation. Some brave critics, such as Brian Millar writing in 2015 in *Parapsychology: A Handbook for the 21st Century*, concede, "There is . . . some truth in the New Age canard." Indeed, one hears a lot less complaining from the mainstream today than say, fifteen or twenty years ago, about mystical interpretations of quantum theory. This is not because we as a human community have grown tired of complaining (our ever-renewable resource). It is because, similar to the UFO thesis (and I hope soon the ESP thesis), the center has moved closer to the metaphysical interpretation.

Indeed, the implications of quantum data are increasingly important because we are encountering *parallel insights* in other sciences. This returns us to the field of neuroplasticity. Researchers in neuroplasticity use brain scans to demonstrate that thought—a familiar word of which we do not possess a clear definition, even as we advance toward concepts of artificial intelligence—actually alters the neural pathways through which electrical impulses travel in the brain. This results in changes of targeted behaviors, including in areas of addiction and obsessive-compulsive disorder (OCD).

One of the field's pioneers, UCLA research psychiatrist Jeffrey M. Schwartz wrote, "I propose that the time has come for science to confront serious implications of the fact that directed, willed mental activity can clearly and systematically alter brain function; that the exertion of willful effort generates a *physical force* that has the power to change how the brain works and even its physical structure."

Schwartz linked his UCLA findings to developments in quantum physics. "The implications of direct neuroplasticity combined with quantum physics," he observed in his 2002 book *The Mind and the Brain*, "cast new light on the question of humanity's place, and role, in nature." The co-emergence of the two fields, Schwartz argued, "suggests that the natural world evolves through an interplay between two causal processes."

If thought can alter neural pathways, and affect corresponding behaviors, then brain biology must be understood as the *product of thought* as much as the other way around. This process, Schwartz wrote, "allows human thoughts to make a difference in the evolution of physical events."

Hence, I am engaging in more than metaphor when I speak of rhythmic correspondences, sensory measurements, and mental selectivity. All of this suggests that we are, in some very real respects, *protean beings*—participants in self-creation—and to a far greater degree than has been commonly understood or acknowledged.

*   *   *

With that contention made, let me return to the practical mechanics of mind causation. I believe that nothing on the path does more to stifle your sense of morale, purpose, possibility, and selfhood than being told what you are *supposed* to find or how you are supposed to live or what your spiritual values are supposed to be or what the search is supposed to be about. Self-determination is vital to everything I have been describing. Including if it contradicts my proclivities.

In my observation, the ability to direct your mental-emotive energies requires a measure of assurance and hopeful expectancy. This is commonly observed in placebo studies. The belief that something *can happen*—and that your mind plays an extra-cognitive role in this—is critical. Another elusive concept, *faith*, is an umbrella term for these catalytic factors. We often define faith or hope as a belief that all will turn out right in the end. In actuality, I do not possess that outlook or temperament. If anything, I have struggled my entire life with anxiety. This is probably why I dedicated myself to the field of positive-mind metaphysics. I have never really suffered from depression but anxiety can get its claws in me at 4 a.m. when I ought to be sleeping but my mind and emotions are racing. Years ago, I delivered a talk at a wealthy retirement community in New York's Hudson Valley. After I finished, an audience member approached me and asked, "How do you sleep at night?" At first, I thought I had offended her. I then realized what she meant. "Your brain," she continued, "it's always going." She was right. "Oh yeah, that's true," I said. "I actually don't sleep very much." So, that's my struggle. Then where does a sense of hopeful expectancy come from? How does faith or great expectation enter the picture?

In my observation, faith is bound up with, and in some ways equivalent to, persistence. *Meaningful persistence* is faith. That is the experience described in the story of the pink, heart-shaped buckets. My effort did not involve optimism. Unless you call it *optimism of the will* to use the term attributed to revolutionary political theorist Antonio Gramsci.* Through passion of dedication, my full psyche was in play. The psyche is a compact of *thought and emotion.*

It is important to note that thoughts, emotions, and physicality run on separate tracks. They are distinct forces. If thoughts ruled us, no one would have a problem with anger, addiction, overeating, and so on. Your thoughts would suffice to curb the unwanted consumption or outburst. Emotion and physicality are often stronger than thought. Hence, we can seldom talk ourselves out of a mood or craving. We can use our minds (which run on a continuum with spirituality) to help circumvent mood or craving; but those things are enormously powerful and they sometimes must receive their due. They run on their own tracks and are owed something. Moods and cravings are not just to be corralled and reorganized; they may have a valid claim on us. I point this out simply to highlight that thought is not the only mediator of power.

As an amalgam of thought and emotion, the unified psyche is powerful: it is the totality of your psychology. This compact forms only when you progress in the direction of a passionately felt need. That is why I consider desires sacred; they are key to human growth and

---

* Gramsci adopted the phrase "pessimism of the intellect, optimism of the will" from French political writer Romain Rolland. Gramsci reflected poignantly on the concept in a letter written from prison in December 1929: "[A] man ought to be so deeply convinced that the source of his own moral forces is in himself...that he never despairs and never falls into those vulgar, banal moods, pessimism and optimism. My own state of mind synthesizes these two feelings and transcends them: *my mind is pessimistic, but my will is optimistic* [emphasis added]. Since I never build up illusions, I am seldom disappointed. I've always been armed with unlimited patience—not a passive, inert kind, but a patience allied with perseverance." Quoted from "On Revolutionary Optimism of the Intellect" by Leo Panitch, *Socialist Register*, Vol. 53, 2017.

striving. A desire does not necessarily liberate you from things that are *owed to others*. But a desire points you in the direction of authenticity. As such, a desire should be carefully understood and, whenever principle permits, heeded. Do not allow a noninvasive desire to get taken from you. Desire must not be taken away because *persistence in its direction summons the forces called faith, expectation, belief in self, and investment in the greater possibility of the individual.*

That which you experience with your whole psyche, and move toward in every effortful way, sets in motion the pendulum effect I described. Barring some countervailing force, this motion, like a bow pulled and released, lawfully swings in the direction of what is focused on. Again, these are not random metaphors. I am describing concepts that appear in Hermeticism and that find shared insights in the scientific fields I have referenced and will further. These concepts are also warranted by seekers across centuries. I have provided you with a testimony of my own.

*   *   *

I have not forgotten about my self-selected interlocutor, philosopher Christopher Lasch. If causative mental agencies are more than escapist fantasy, or an expression of secondary narcissism as Lasch suggested, how does that prospect relate to the broader challenge the philosopher issued? In the afterword of *The Culture of Narcissism*, Lasch sharpened his critique of religious or social models that extol gratification—and pointed to his vision of a sounder, stabler approach to life. He observed compellingly:

The best hope of emotional maturity, then, appears to lie in a recognition of our need for and dependence on people who nevertheless remain separate from ourselves and refuse to submit to our whims. It lies in a recognition of others not as projections of our own desires but as independent beings with desires of their own. More broadly, it lies in acceptance of our limits. The world does not exist merely to satisfy our own desires; it is a world in which we can find pleasure and meaning, once we understand that others too have a right to these goods. Psychoanalysis confirms the ancient religious insight that the only way to achieve happiness is to accept limitations in a spirit of gratitude and contrition instead of attempting to annul those limitations or bitterly resenting them.

My wish is not to foster an imagined escape from life's obligations or a justification to bend others to our desires. Indeed, the chief sign of weakness masquerading as agency is when someone continually burdens others to repair his moods, support his psyche, or dispense rewards. Nor am I positing a system without limits or barriers. Unwillingness to bow to or acknowledge frustrations can become a form of theater in which the indestructible being conceals his or her own lack of self-belief.

In the *Corpus Hermeticum*—the primary body of Greek Hermetic texts translated during the Renaissance— humanity, for all its potential greatness, is conscripted to dwell within a framework where physical laws must be suffered. The individual is at once a being of boundless potential and natural limits—a paradox that creates the tension of existence.

"The master of eternity," reads the dialogue called *Asclepius*, "is the first god, the world"—or great nature—"is second, mankind is the third."* In the Hermetic framing, man, a being ever in the state of advancing or becoming, is considered superior to the gods, whose existence is fixed; but man in his present mode of living nonetheless remains subservient to coarser aspects of nature.

Book I of the *Corpus Hermeticum* teaches: "mankind is affected by mortality because he is subject to fate"—fate is a term for nature's governance—"thus, although man is above the cosmic framework, he became a slave within it." In Hermetic teaching man's mystic prowess is bound by organic tethers.

I believe in experiential philosophies that elevate and encourage our expansion toward self-expression and heightened existence—without denying existential trauma. Such outlooks bring purpose, intention, striving, focus, and *beingness* to our existence. The philosophy of mind causation, on the terms explored here, not only abets authentic selfhood but forms its foundation.

As I see it, nothing in this approach abrogates or fundamentally conflicts with Lasch's analysis, other than his blanket disparagement of New Age. More importantly, the mind causation thesis contributes a defensibly greater possibility to the human situation than what appears in Lasch's or many other secular psycho-social outlooks. As

---

* I am quoting from Brian P. Copenhaver's seminal translation, *Hermetica* (Cambridge University Press, 1992).

seeking people, we must avoid delusional excesses, which occur on *either extreme*—mystical or materialist—of how one views the psyche.

Within New Age culture, as Lasch justly critiques, we are often conditioned to think in elusive or inflated concepts of self-development and its horizons. People of a spiritual orientation might use terms like *realized, enlightened,* or *illumined.* I find such language excessive. People of a psychological bent might use terms like *well-adjusted, actualized,* or *fulfilled.* Those concepts are more graspable; but, like the vocabulary of cognitive-behavioral therapy, psychological terminology can proscribe the individual to a life of diagnostic contentment rather than support a more expansive sense of attainment. I reaffirm my contention that *the true aim of life is self-expression.* And we possess tools—including mind causation—in that effort. Such prospects are not to everyone's spiritual and ethical tastes but nor do they require a break with philosophical sobriety.

It may be asked whether personal guardrails are necessary to prevent the effort I describe from resulting in exploitation of others or despotic "reality distortion." In that vein, I am inspired by a principle from Ralph Waldo Emerson's journals of January 15, 1827:

> The nature of God may be different from what he is represented. I never beheld him. I do not know that he exists. This good which invites me now is visible & specific. I will at least embrace it this time by way of experiment, & if it is wrong certainly God can in some manner signify his will in future. Moreover I

will guard against evil consequences resulting to others by the vigilance with which I conceal it.

You alone are responsible for your experiments: not every impulse requires acting on or revealing; certain wishes must be abided in quiet; certain are to be considered from the scale of reciprocity and debts owed. Here I am reminded of a statement by philosopher and critic of science Paul Feyerabend: "I am for anarchism in *thinking*, in one's *private life*, BUT NOT in *public life*."* I have no right to demand that another person or institution mirror my self-conception. But I commit an equal violation if I do not know myself and exercise the full faculties of my psyche.

*   *   *

I have insisted that self-expression is critical to a satisfying—if not unerringly successful—existence. I believe that paucity of self-expression results in anxiety, depression, ennui, addiction, and is often diagnosed and coded in the therapist's office without this factor—the power and agency intrinsic to self-expression—named or acknowledged. In that sense, I am more a child of the sixties and seventies, perhaps, than Lasch would approve. He writes, "The best defenses against the terrors of existence are the homely comforts of love, work, and family life, which connect us to a world that is independent of our wishes yet responsive to our needs."

---

* *Against Method*, fourth edition by Paul Feyerabend (Verso, 1975, 1988, 1993, 2010)

The philosopher's biographer Eric Miller calls Lasch's writing his "most fundamental vocational impulse" and "enduring passion," describing the prodigy authoring his "first complete book" by age eleven.* So I ask: would Lasch, denied the writer's pen, the teacher's lectern, the public's ear, have found sufficient defense in those "homely comforts?"

One area where the philosopher and I soundly agree is when he writes: "We demand too much of life, too little of ourselves." Our values are similar. Our metaphysics are not. I hope that I have responded to Lasch's estimable critique of New Age and modern metaphysics while providing a useful and persuasive counter approach to life.

But I wish to do more than offer a counterview. I also owe it to you as the reader to be defensibly *right* about the powers upon which I urge you to draw. The best way I know to assess this prospect is by exploring the branch of science dedicated to studying and documenting extraphysicality and the force of thought: parapsychology, to which we now turn.

---

* *Hope In a Scattering Time: A Life of Christopher Lasch* by Eric Miller (Eerdmans, 2010)

Chapter Twelve

The Parapsychology Revolution

arapsychology is a young science. But its march forward marks a seismic change in our world—and our view of ourselves. In this chapter, which is a tonal departure from some of the more personal or practical ones in the book, I hope to introduce the inception and advances of psychical research, the barriers it faces, and the extraordinary and unlikely victories the field has attained in expanding our conception of human nature and possibilities. (Since this chapter is driven less by experience than data, and my interpretation of it, it is also extensively footnoted; the footnotes are intended to provide a journey in themselves.)

I believe that our culture is poised for an epochal change in how we understand and accept the core findings of parapsychology—that is, acceptance of the empiricism of the extra-physical. Rejectionism tends to harden on the brink of seismic change, and we are seeing pockets of that, as well. Indeed, some voices of denialism will never acknowledge evidence for immaterial experience no matter how successfully validated and replicated. That is, in a sense, unimportant to individual development; but broadening our knowledge pool is important to our growth as a human community. Hence, my approach is not to persuade committed rejectionists but to inure our excellence as a seeking generation—and then move on without them.

The outcome of the present moment is, I believe, general acknowledgment that we as a global culture possess indelible evidence of an extra-physical component to life. The vistas of advancement that lay beyond that acknowledgment pose extraordinary questions, which may alter our view of human nature as much as Darwinism did in the Victorian age.

*   *   *

I often speak of a "Parapsychology Revolution." It is a quiet and long-simmering revolution in the modern era. When occult scholar Manly P. Hall published his landmark study of esotericism *The Secret Teachings of All Ages* in 1928, no mention of parapsychology appeared in the book. German philosopher and psychologist Max Dessoir (1867–1947) coined the term *parapsychologie* in 1889 to describe empirical study of extra-physical phenomena, including clairvoyance, mediumship, precognition, and after-death survival, but the concept was not yet widely known.

"Organized psychical research can be dated, symbolically, from a conversation between Henry Sidgwick and his student F.W.H. Myers, one moonlit night in Cambridge about 1870, over the need to validate religious belief through the methods of empirical science," wrote historians Seymour H. Mauskopf and Michael R. McVaugh in their valuable study of psi research, *The Elusive Science*.

The more formal scientific scrutiny of anomalous phenomena marked its starting point in 1882 when the Society for Psychical Research (SPR) was founded in London by scientists including Myers (who coined the term telepathy for mind-to-mind communication) and pioneering psychologist and philosopher William James—and included a remarkable array of clinical luminaries, such as physicist Oliver Lodge, Sigmund Freud (a member of both the British and American chapters), economist and ethical philosopher Henry Sidgwick, and Arthur Balfour, Britain's prime minister from 1902 to 1905.

At its inception, parapsychology sought to test mediumistic phenomena under controlled conditions. The early SPR worked with rigor to hold spirit mediums to proof. Researchers such as the strong-willed Richard Hodgson and James himself ventured to the séance table intent on safeguarding against fraud and documenting claimed phenomena, including physical mediumship, after-death communication, and clairvoyance or what is today called channeling. (The twentieth-century medical psychic Edgar Cayce first used the term "channel" in a metaphysical sense.) They probed unexplained cases, exposed frauds, and created historical controversies that have lingered until today. But they were functioning largely within the lace-curtained settings of Victorian parlors. On the whole, SPR researchers were not operating in clinical environments, so-called white coat lab settings where an atmosphere of experimenter control abetted seeking evidence for extra-physical phenomena, whether in statistical patterns or recording of events. The American chapter of the SPR, meanwhile, grew stymied by factional disputes between members more interested in the after-death survival thesis and those committed to the more conservative direction of documenting mental phenomena.

I do not intend to leave the impression that lab-based study of psychical phenomena was absent. In the 1880s, Nobel laureate and SPR president Charles Richet, one of France's most highly regarded biologists, studied telepathy with subjects under hypnosis. Richet also introduced the use of statistical analysis in ESP card tests, presaging today's near-universal use of statistics throughout the psychological and social sciences.* In the early 1920s, French engineer René Warcollier conducted a series of experiments on long-distance telepathy. Freud himself, often seen as a rationalist counterpart to his more occult-leaning former disciple Carl Jung, publicly and privately pondered the possibilities of telepathy, sometimes delaying publication of key statements posthumously to avoid professional fallout. This was the case with Freud's

---

* See "Telepathy: Origins of Randomization in Experimental Design" by Ian Hacking, *Isis*, Sept 1988, Vol. 79, No. 3; "J. B. Rhine's *Extra-Sensory Perception* and Its Background in Psychical Research" by Michael McVaugh and Seymour H. Mauskopf, *Isis*, June 1976, Vol. 67, No. 2; and "Charles Richet" by C.S. Alvarado, *Psi Encyclopedia*, London: The Society for Psychical Research, 2015.

"Psychoanalysis and Telepathy," his earliest paper on the topic written in 1921—but withheld from publication until 1941, two years after his death.* (This was likely at the urging of his English biographer Ernest Jones, who found the topic professionally compromising.**) Freud's first published statement on ESP appeared in the more reserved essay "Dreams and Telepathy" in 1922, where he observed: "Psychoanalysis may do something to advance the study of telepathy, in so far as, by the help of its interpretations, many of the puzzling characteristics of telepathic phenomena may be rendered more intelligible to use; or other, still doubtful phenomena be for the first time definitely ascertained to be of a telepathic nature."

Another decade passed before study of the paranormal burgeoned into an acknowledged, if hotly debated, academic field. This was due largely to ESP researcher J.B. Rhine (1895–1980) and his wife and intellectual partner Louisa Rhine (1891–1983). In the late 1920s and early 30s, the Rhines established the research program that became the Parapsychology Laboratory at Duke University in Durham, North Carolina, which made paradigmatic advances in the scientific study of ESP. A generation on, ardent skeptics rolled back the Rhines' progress in the public and academic mind, a topic this chapter also considers.

---

* The history of the paper appears in a critical postscript to its publication in volume 18 of *The Standard Edition of the Complete Psychological Works of Sigmund Freud*, published in 1955.

** "I am extremely sorry that my utterance about telepathy should have plunged you into fresh difficulties," Freud wrote to Jones in 1925. "But it is really hard not to offend English sensibilities . . ." For a revealing and sometimes-humorous exchange of their letters on the topic, see *The Future of the Body* by Michael Murphy (Jeremy P. Tarcher, 1992) and volume 3 of Jones's *The Life and Work of Sigmund Freud* (Basic Books, 1957).

J.B. and Louisa trained as statisticians and botanists at the University of Chicago where both received doctorates, a considerable rarity for a woman then. In the 1920s, botanists were considered at the forefront of statistical theory. While at Chicago in 1922, they were inspired by a talk on Spiritualism by English author Arthur Conan Doyle. Although taken by Doyle's "utter sincerity," J.B. later feuded with the writer over the deceptions of one of Doyle's favored mediums.* With J.B.'s eyes on greater horizons, he soon grew restless in his chosen career. "It would be unpardonable for the scientific world today to overlook evidences of the supernormal in our world," J.B. told what must have been a mildly surprised audience of scientific agriculturalists in spring of 1926 at the University of West Virginia, where he held a teaching position.**

The Rhines began casting around, venturing to Columbia University and Harvard, seeking opportunities to combine their scientific training with the metaphysical interests that had ignited their relationship as adolescents. J.B. and Louisa met with some attention and encouragement but progress proved fitful. Odd jobs were necessary to stay afloat. Children were soon on the horizon, with the first of four, a boy, adopted in early 1929 after the death of

---

* *Something Hidden* by Louisa E. Rhine (McFarland, 1983)

** For this quote and the next see *The Elusive Science: Origins of Experimental Psychical Research* by Seymour H. Mauskopf and Michael R. McVaugh with an afterword by J.B. and L.E. Rhine (The Johns Hopkins University Press, 1980). This seminal historical text—the finest of its kind in my reading—is unfortunately out of print and of limited availability of as this writing: it is a situation that I hope a scholarly or trade press remedies.

a premature newborn, and three daughters born through 1934.*

"I think, too, we are tiring of chasing the Psychic rainbow or the Philosophic pot of gold," J.B. wrote in his notes in January of 1927. As often occurs in life, just prior to resignation following immense effort, an extraordinary— and in this case, historic—opportunity appeared. The new chairman of Duke's psychology department, William McDougall—a past president of both the American and British SPR who favored scientifically driven research of mental phenomena—encouraged the Rhines in their work, bringing the couple to Durham that fall. In 1930, with the support of Duke's first president, William Preston Few, McDougall made J.B. Rhine a formal part of the campus.** Although the founding of Duke's Parapsychology Laboratory is often dated to that year, J.B.'s program

---

* See *J.B. Rhine, Letters 1923-1939* edited by Barbara Ensrud and Sally Rhine Feather (McFarland, 2021) and *J.B. Rhine: On the Frontiers of Science* edited by K. Ramakrishna Rao (McFarland, 1982).

** Few was an interesting figure himself. He had been president of Duke in its earlier incarnation as Trinity College, a Methodist school, and he oversaw its growth, transformation, and renaming in 1924 in honor of its benefactors. Few was eager to establish Duke's reputation and saw J.B. Rhine as part of that effort. To Few, the erudite and energetic researcher might someday write something to "top [William] James' *Varieties of Religious Experience*." Few's wife was personally interested in ESP and two of Duke's trustees were active dowsers (an occult water-seeking practice with deep roots in the American south) and supported his work. "This firm administrative support of ESP," wrote Mauskopf and McVaugh, "had many tangible consequences: provision of a secretary to handle Rhine's correspondence; the establishment of special laboratory quarters for Rhine's staff when the psychology department moved into a new building in the summer of 1935; and steady promotion and raises in salary for Rhine himself." Since this is, in part, a practical book, I will add a related note: Dedicate your labor where you are most valued. You cannot succeed in a two-front war where you are simultaneously trying to do your best work and win over recalcitrant sponsors or employers.

was not christened the Parapsychology Laboratory until 1935 (in 1929 he called his prototype the "Institute for Experimental Religion"), where it remained until 1965. Today, the Rhine Research Center continues as an independent lab off campus. In all, it proved a watershed episode in which parapsychology was formally folded into an academic structure and study of the psychical became a profession.

At Duke, J.B. did not quite originate but popularized the phrase extrasensory perception, or ESP, which soon became a household term. The work begun at Duke's Parapsychology Lab in the early 1930s—which I will soon revisit—has continued among different researchers, labs, and universities to the present day. The effort is to provide impeccably documented evidence that human beings participate in some form of existence that exceeds cognition, motor skill, and commonly observed biological functions—that we participate in trackable, replicable patterns of extra-physicality that permit us, at least sometimes, to communicate and receive information in a manner that surpasses generally acknowledged sensory experience and means of data conveyance. This field of exchange occurs independently of time, space, or mass.

We have also accumulated a body of statistical evidence for psychokinesis (i.e., mind over matter) and precognition or what is sometimes called retrocausality, in which events in the future affect the present. An example of the latter may involve cases in which present activities, such as memorization of a word list, are positively and measurably impacted—in a replicable manner using widely accepted statistical models—based on actions that have *not yet occurred*, such as near-future study of that list.* For several years, Dean Radin, chief scientist at the Institute of Noetic Sciences (IONS) in Northern California, has performed and replicated experiments in precognition in which subjects display bodily stressors, such as pupil dilation or increased heart rate, seconds before being shown distressing or emotionally triggering imagery.**

We likewise possess evidence of traumatic or otherwise notable global events, such as the terrorist attacks of 9/11, producing statistical deviations in expected random outputs in machinery called random number generators or random event generators.*** Random number generators emit infinite patterns of chaotic numbers without order. This technology is often used to devise online passwords. Scientists at the now-retired Princeton Engineering Anomalies Research Lab (PEAR), founded in 1979 by Princeton's dean of engineering, Robert G. Jahn, and presently under the auspices of the Global Consciousness Project, have documented periods of worldwide global emotional intensity—other examples include the elections

---

* A recent precognition study that we will soon consider appears in "Feeling the Future: Experimental Evidence for Anomalous Retroactive Influences on Cognition and Affect" by Daryl J. Bem, *Journal of Personality and Social Psychology*, 2011, Vol. 100, No. 3.

** See: "Time-reversed human experience: Experimental evidence and implications" by Dean Radin, Esalen Draft, 7/31/00, https://www.researchgate.net/publication/239611072_Time-reversed_human_experience_Experimental_evidence_and_implications and "Intuition Through Time: What Does the Seer See?" by Dean Radin, Ph.D., and Ana Borges, J.D., *Explore*, 2009; Vol 5, No. 4. For a meta-analysis of recent precognition experiments see "Precognition as a form of prospection: A review of the evidence" by Julia A. Mossbridge and Dean Radin, *Psychology of Consciousness: Theory, Research, and Practice*, March 2018, Vol 5, No. 1.

*** E.g., https://noosphere.princeton.edu/exploratory.analysis.html

of Barack Obama and Donald Trump—during which random number generators placed in select locations around the world demonstrate inexplicable patterns, or interruptions in randomness, during spikes of highly focused human attention.* "Periods of collective attention or emotion in widely distributed populations will correlate with deviations from expectation in a global network of physical random number generators," the researchers wrote in their test hypothesis.** Patterns (sometimes slight, other times more pronounced) appear where none should; there ought to be perfect chaos. The data suggests, at least as a proposition, that we as a human species produce some manner of psychokinetic (PK) signal or disruptive awareness during episodes of mass emotional intensity.

These are fleeting references to a handful of recent findings from modern parapsychology. I am going to make a statement and I am then going to argue for it. My statement is simple. *We possess heavily scrutinized, replicable statistical evidence for an extra-physical component of the human psyche.* For decades, this evidence has appeared in—and been reproduced for—traditional, academically based journals, often juried by scientists without sympathy in the direction of its findings. This evidence has been procured and replicated under rigorous clinical conditions. It demonstrates that the individual possesses or participates in a facet of existence that surpasses what is known to us biologically, psychologically, sensorily, and technologically. In short: ESP exists.

---

* E.g., https://noosphere.princeton.edu/results.html#alldata

** https://noosphere.princeton.edu/abstract.html

*　　*　　*

What I am describing is, in a sense, nothing new since recorded mystical experience extending to time imme- morial has affirmed some of these points. Indeed, many of you reading these words have had exceptional or extraordinary experiences, which left an indelible mark on your life. These experiences occurred against all rea- sonable odds, even if we account for the aforementioned "law of large numbers." To recap from the chapter on prayer, the law of large numbers says, in effect, that since ours is a big planet it follows that strange or seemingly impossible things must happen to *someone*. But that rationalist or, as it is more often used, materialist expla- nation has lapses: specifically, when an event proves repeatable—entering a statistically rarified strata that belies randomness—or when an apparently chance event is so deeply steeped in emotional or intimate relevancy to the individual that its meaning exceeds measurable odds.* Withholding certainty in the face of such expe- riences attaches you to a chain of seekers that extends back millennia. Suspension of certainty is the line that separates cynics from skeptics. True skeptics question; cynics reach for solutions that remind them most readily of themselves or of what they feel threatened by. Hence,

---

* I cited two examples earlier: 1) when skeptic Michael Shermer described uncanny occurrences that evoked a deceased family relation on his wedding day: "Anomalous Events That Can Shake One's Skepticism to the Core," *Scientific American* column, October 2014, and 2) my "pink buckets" episode in the previous chapter. Shermer and I, writing in the same year—my story in my book *One Simple Idea* in January 2014 and his column in October 2014— reached essentially the same conclusion.

their haste to assign motives of self-interest or to express contempt for the questioner.

The search for greater dimensions of life, and one's connection to them, are inseparable from the human situation. Once primeval humanity had attended to reproduction, shelter, hunting, and agriculture, the activity that established human beings on this planet was the search for the greater. As alluded earlier, in the Negev Desert sit remains of an altar thought to be dedicated to worshiping the moon and estimated at 25,000 years old. This and other sites reflect primordial humanity in some of its earliest expressions. Following the basics of survival, humanity sought connection to the greater, the cosmic, the numinous.

Hence, my contentions are as old as humanity itself. But what is new and revolutionary is *the advent of science as a method of protocols to identify processes that affirm primordial humanity's basic instinct for the extra-physical.* As noted, this places our generation before a remarkable precipice. It is one that we have not yet been able to cross. The precipice is that the philosophy called materialism, by which Western life has largely been organized for more than 200 years, is facing obsolescence. Philosophical materialism holds that matter creates itself. And that your mind is strictly an epiphenomenon of your brain. That thoughts are a localized function of gray matter which, like bubbles in a glass of carbonated water, are gone once the water is gone. And that is the extent of the psyche. That philosophy is defunct. Its obsolescence is due not only to the amassing of data verifying the extra-physical—gathered through the same methodology that materialism purports to defend—but also to the progressing realization that materialism is simply a position, a theory, an ideology, of which science is independent.

Materialism has accompanied the scientific method to such an extent that it appears joined to it—and, among its defenders, materialism actually surpasses science, as they deny clinical evidence in contradiction to it. But materialism is simply a modernist theory and not a rationalist imperative. This does not mean that materialism will fade gently. Its outlook—that matter evinces no calculable reality beyond classical mechanics and that all contrary evidence or implications are false because they contradict its founding premise—will retain influence for decades. The materialist perspective is concretized within key parts of our culture and media and is held to with conviction by many opinion-shaping personalities. Its very obsolescence explains much of the overwrought pushback and even rhetorical disingenuousness deployed against countervailing data from parapsychology. Indeed, materialist dominance inevitably slackens as greater evidence of the extra-physical comes to light with no attendant compromise of progress in terms of technology, medicine, velocity, coding, or communication. In fact, all of those things are accelerated because we come to realize that the nature of the psyche surpasses our estimates, which opens new vistas of query.*

---

* Although it goes beyond the breadth of this chapter, most of the founders of quantum theory were philosophical idealists, i.e., they interpreted and documented a naturalistic universe that includes, and is affected by, laws of perception. "This demonstrates that world-class science—science that created the modern world—was actually performed on an entirely different set of worldview assumptions," Dean Radin remarked to me on December 31, 2021. Indeed,

*   *   *

I have ventured several bold statements. So, let me dial things back for a moment. Now that I have made my big-picture contention, it behooves me to support my points. What evidence exists for my chin-out claims of science affirming the infinite? Here I return to Duke's Parapsychology Laboratory in the early 1930s. J.B. Rhine's innovation as a researcher is that he wanted to develop clear, repeatable, and unimpeachable methods, with rigor and without drama or speculation, for testing and statistically mapping evidence for anomalous communication and conveyance. To attempt this, Rhine initially created a series of card-guessing tests that involved a deck called Zener cards designed by psychologist Karl E. Zener (1903–1964). You may recall seeing Zener card tests affectionately lampooned in the opening scene of *Ghostbusters*. (Cowriter and costar Dan Ackroyd is a lifelong aficionado of the paranormal.) Zener cards are a five-suit deck, generally with 25 cards in a pack, with symbols that are easily and immediately recognizable: circle, square, cross, wavy lines, and five-pointed star. After a deck is shuffled, subjects are asked to attempt blind hits on what symbol will turn up.

Over time, and across tens of thousands of trials, guesswork will produce a one-in-five or 20 percent hit

the "father of quantum physics," Max Planck (1858–1947) observed: "All matter originates and exists only by virtue of a force which brings the particle of an atom to vibration and holds this most minute solar system of the atom together. We must assume behind this force the existence of a conscious and intelligent mind. This mind is the matrix of all matter." And elsewhere: "I regard matter as derived from consciousness." See "Quantum mechanics and the consciousness connection" by Susan Borowski, *Scientia blog*, 7/16/2012, American Association for the Advancement of Science.

rate. At a certain point, these odds are lawful. We no longer speak in terms of a "law of statistics" or "law of averages;" those concepts are considered colloquial, and understandably so because they are often misunderstood and misapplied in gambling situations. But across the span of extremely large numbers that colloquialism holds true. Probability dictates that over large spreads you are going to hit 20 percent, or one out of five, if you are operating from random chance. But Rhine discovered, across literally tens and eventually hundreds of thousands of rigorously safeguarded trials (by 1940, the database included nearly a million trials*) that certain individuals, rather than scoring 20 percent would score 25 percent, 26 percent, 27 percent, sometimes 28 percent (and in select cases a great deal higher).** All of the data were reported. Nothing was withheld in the "file drawer," so to speak. No negative sets were excluded. At the time, social scientists across the field commonly withheld negative sets on the questionable grounds that something was flawed with the methodology. Rhine reversed this practice early on at his lab and helped lead the overall social sciences to do so.***

---

* "Who Was J.B. Rhine?" by Rick Berger, Ph.D., February 14, 2020, at parapsych.org, website of the Parapsychological Association.

** E.g., see *Extra-Sensory Perception* by J.B. Rhine (1934, Boston Society for Psychic Research).

*** E.g., see "Editorial" by Gardner Murphy and Bernard F. Riess, *The Journal of Parapsychology*, June 1939, Vol 3, No. 1, in which the authors review Rhine's protocols. In an age of "anything goes" verbiage online, few of us realize the sacrifices entailed in meaningfully heterodox expression. The co-writer of this editorial, Bernard F. Riess was, with Gardner Murphy, not only co-editor of *The Journal of Parapsychology* from 1939 to 1941, but a respected psychologist who in 1952 lost his teaching position at Hunter College in New York City for refusing to answer questions about his political beliefs and affiliations in front of a Senate committee during the McCarthy Era. "He felt he had a

Hence, the pooled data displayed inexplicable deviations of sometimes just a few percentage points, but repeatedly and demonstrably above chance possibility. In a related landmark, the first modern meta-analysis, in which data from varied experiments are analyzed, validated (or identified as flawed), and statistically mapped, appeared in Rhine's 1940 monograph, *Extra-Sensory Perception After Sixty Years*, a topic to which I return. The term "meta-analysis" itself was not coined until 1976.

In the footsteps of his establishment of transparent protocols and pooled data, Rhine also included an estimate of how *unpublished* papers would impact overall effects—this relates to the so-called file drawer problem or "publication bias" in favor of results, a common procedural and ethical lapse in the social sciences. "Such private information as can be assembled regarding unpublished work," Rhine and his collaborators wrote in *Extra-Sensory Perception after Sixty Years*, ". . . shows that by a large majority, the unpublished reports are favorable to ESP rather than nonconfirmatory." For many academic researchers, claims of ESP were more daunting than the opposite.

In Rhine's work, every precaution was taken against corruption, withholding, or pollution of data, which was also opened to other researchers (and non-research-based critics) for replication, vetting, and review. In a letter of March 15, 1960, to mathematician and foundation exec-

---

right to his belief in Marxism," his son John said. "He also didn't want to be in a position of having to incriminate others." See "Dr. Bernard F. Riess, 87, Who Lost Teaching Post in McCarthy Era" by Robert D. McFadden, *New York Times*, July 10, 1995.

utive Warren Weaver, Rhine referenced the extra lengths to which the parapsychologist ought to go: "Even though the methodology and standards of evidence may compare favorably with other advances of natural science, they have to be superior in parapsychology because of its novelty; and conceivably, too, by making them still better, everything may be gained in overcoming the natural resistance involved."*

The "natural resistance" or partisanship around such findings can be so intense—and sometimes purposefully obfuscating or confusing—that even well-intentioned lay seekers come away with the impression that Rhine's work, or that of more recent parapsychologists, has proven unrepeatable or compromised. The parapsychologist Charles Honorton, about whom more will be heard, sought to analyze critical challenges to Rhine's figures in the years following their publication. In his 1975 presidential address to the Parapsychological Association, a professional society for parapsychologists, Honorton said:

> Even among parapsychologists there is a rather widespread belief that most of the independent replication of the early Duke work were non-confirmatory and I suspect this may be especially true among those of us who were not around in the 1930's (which, incidentally, accounts for about three-fourths of the participants at this convention). In fact, I was surprised myself to find that this wasn't so when I

---

* Rhine's letter is from the Parapsychology Laboratory Records, 1893–1984, Rare Book, Manuscript, and Special Collections Library, Duke University, Durham, NC.

undertook a review of all the English-language ESP experiments reported during the period between 1934 and 1939.*

Honorton's effort involved a database of about 3.3 million individual trials. He described further:

During the five-year period following publication of J.B. Rhine's *Extra-Sensory Perception* in 1934, the scientific community responded as it should to any claim of new discovery, by disseminating both positive and negative research findings, by careful scrutiny of the experimental and evaluative techniques, and by encouraging fresh replication efforts. During this period there were approximately 60 critical articles by 40 authors, published primarily in the American psychological literature. Fifty experimental studies were reported during this period, two-thirds of which represented independent replication efforts by other laboratories of the Duke University work.

Honorton found that "61 percent of the independent replications of the Duke work were statistically significant. This is 60 times the proportion of significant studies we would expect if the significant results were due to chance or error." In 2020, parapsychologist Rick Berger, Ph.D., broke down the figures further for the Parapsychological Association: "In the five years following Rhine's first

* "Has Science Developed the Competence to Confront the Paranormal?" by Charles Honorton, *Extrasensory Perception*, Vol. 2, edited by Edwin C. May and Sonali Bhatt Marwaha (Praeger, 2015)

publication of his results, 33 independent replication experiments were conducted at different laboratories. Twenty (20) of these (or 61%) were statistically significant (where 5% would be expected by chance alone)." *

Rhine's experiments have proven sufficiently bulletproof so that even close to fifty years later his most resistant critics were still attempting to explain them by fantastical (and often feckless) fraud theories, including a prominent English skeptic's nearly vaudevillian supposition that one of the test subjects repeatedly crawled through a ceiling space to peek at cards through a trapdoor over the lab.** At such excesses, rationalists fail the test that Enlightenment philosopher David Hume (1711–1776) set for validation of miracles: counterclaims must be less likely than reported phenomena. In any case, Rhine's methods and results have never been upended.

For all that, Rhine may have proven too idealistic regarding what it took to overcome "natural resistance." I referred earlier to "overwrought pushback and even rhetorical disingenuousness deployed against countervailing data from parapsychology." A prime example appears in how polemical skeptics today ride herd over

---

* "Who Was J.B. Rhine?," February 14, 2020, at parapsych.org, website of the Parapsychological Association. Additional replication and detailed examination of every contemporaneous criticism appears in *Extra-Sensory Perception After Sixty Years* by J.G. Pratt, J.B. Rhine, Burke M. Smith, Charles E. Stuart, and Joseph A. Greenwood (Henry Holt, 1940).

** See *ESP and Parapsychology: A Critical Re-Evaluation* by C.E.M. Hansel (Prometheus Books, 1980); "Rhetoric over substance: the impoverished state of skepticism" by Charles Honorton, *Journal of Parapsychology*, June 1993; and Stacy Horn's invaluable study of the Rhine labs, *Unbelievable* (HarperCollins/ Ecco, 2009).

articles on parapsychology on the most-read reference source in history, Wikipedia. As of this writing, Wikipedia's article on Zener cards states in its opening, "The original series of experiments have been discredited and replication has proven elusive." This statement is unsourced, something that would get red-flagged on most of the encyclopedia's articles.*

How does this occur on the world's go-to reference source? Dean Radin, chief scientist at IONS, described to me the problem of an ad hoc group calling itself "Guerrilla Skeptics" policing Wiki entries on parapsychology: "While there are lots of anonymous trolls that have worked hard to trash any Wikipedia pages related to psi, including bios of parapsychologists, this group of extreme skeptics is proudly open that they are rewriting history . . . any

---

* Rhine himself has fared little better on Wikipedia. As of this writing, the biographical article on him is rife with sui generis statements and a plurality of references to books published by Prometheus Books, a Buffalo, New York, press aligned with professional skepticism. The article's declarations are often worded evasively and referenced tautologically, e.g., "It was revealed that Rhine's experiments into extrasensory perception (ESP) contained methodological flaws"—this is footnoted to a book called *Quantum Leaps in the Wrong Direction: Where Real Science Ends . . . and Pseudoscience Begins* by Charles M. Wynn and Arthur W. Wiggins (Joseph Henry Press, 2001), a slender volume with cartoons that lampoons psychical research (and oddly groups Holocaust denial among its topics). Wiki's footnote is keyed to this passage: "[Rhine] suggested that something more than mere guess work was involved in his experiments. He was right! It is now known that the experiments conducted in his laboratory contained serious methodological flaws . . . ," which then misstates Rhine's testing methods from which the authors speculate over frauds, such as "subjects could see card faces reflected in the tester's eyeglasses or cornea." In its review, *Publisher's Weekly* called the sourcebook "lightweight" and concluded, "It won't be long before this title takes a quantum leap into the remainder bins." In another almost humorous passage of the article, professional skeptic Martin Gardner is quoted criticizing Rhine for insufficient disclosure regarding fraud, followed by Gardner's suggestion of his own secret knowledge of compromising files hidden in the Rhine labs. This reflects the present state of crowdsourcing that Wikipedia permits to define Rhine's career.

attempt to edit those pages, even fixing individual words, is blocked or reverted almost instantly." *

I must sometimes smile at the excess of rhetorical brinkmanship in such cases. In the same article in which I quoted Radin, I wrote that the Guerrilla Skeptics "wage a kind of freewheeling digital jihad on Wikipedia." A supporter of the group expressed outrage on Twitter that I would metaphorically call them "jihadists." I pointed out that they call themselves "guerrillas." He insisted that was of no relevance because they were being ironic.

*   *   *

Even if parapsychology as a field had ended with Rhine's initial Duke trials—if no further experiments occurred—we would possess evidence of some sort of paranormal mechanics in human existence. Those basic (though painstakingly structured) card experiments, those few percentage points of deviation tracked across tens of thousands of trials (90,000 in the database by the 1934 publication of *Extra-Sensory Perception*), demonstrate an anomalous transfer of information in a laboratory setting and an extra-physical, call it metaphysical, non-Newtonian exchange of information.

But things did not end there. In the decades ahead, extraordinary waves of diversified experiments occurred in the U.S. and other nations growing from the efforts of the scientists at Duke's Parapsychology Laboratory. These

---

* See my article "The Man Who Destroyed Skepticism," *Boing Boing*, October 26, 2020.

efforts demonstrated, again and again, anomalous mental phenomena, including precognition, retrocausality, telepathy, and psychokinesis (PK). Regarding the last, Rhine's lab began studying PK in 1934, an effort that continued until 1941, after which many lab members were summoned to the war effort. During about nine years of investigation, researchers conducted tens of thousands of runs in which individuals would attempt to affect throws of random sets of dice. Devices were soon employed to toss the dice in such a way that ensured randomness, which ought to demonstrate no pattern whatsoever. Again, similar statistical results to the Zener card experiments appeared: among certain individuals, across hundreds of thousands of throws, with every conceivable safeguard, peer review, methodological transparency, and reportage of every set, there appeared a deviation of several percentage points suggesting a physical effect arising from mental intention.*

We have now logged generations of experiments designed to test the effects to which I am referring. Today's cohort of parapsychologists believes, I think with justification, that the basic, foundational science for psychical ability has already been laid. Although parapsychology remains controversial—about which I will say more—the field has already moved on from basic testing for ESP, a matter that was more or less settled in the 1940s.

---

* See "Chapter 6: Psychokinesis," *An Introduction to Parapsychology*, fifth edition, by Harvey J. Irwin and Caroline A. Watt (McFarland, 2007). Also see www.williamjames.com/Science/PK.htm: "By the end of 1941, a total of 651,216 experimental die throws had been conducted. The combined results of these experiments pointed to a phenomenon with 10,115 to 1 odds against chance occurrence." The Rhines published their initial results in 1943: "The psychokinetic effect: I. The first experiment" by J.B. Rhine and Louisa Rhine, *Journal of Parapsychology* 7.

More recent to our era, researchers are concerned with questions including telepathy, i.e., mind to mind communication; precognition, i.e., the ability to foresee or be affected by things that, within our model of the mind, have not yet occurred; retrocausality, a question related to precognition that hinges on future events affecting current perceptions or abilities; a biological basis for psi (including biologist Rupert Sheldrake's "morphic field" theories); spontaneous psi events, such as premonitions or crisis realizations; dream telepathy; a "global consciousness" effect during periods of mass emotional reaction; and the practice of remote viewing or clairvoyance.* Another critical question is how psychical ability relates to quantum mechanics and whether the latter provides an overall theory of ESP, a topic to which we will return. The field also investigates important areas that surpass my immediate focus here, including out-of-body experiences, near-death experiences, deathbed visions, after-death survival, and reincarnation, the last of which

---

* Although it exceeds the scope of this chapter, there is a great deal of controversy over the CIA-funded remote viewing or "psychic spying" program popularly dubbed the Stargate Project, which in various forms ran from 1972 to 1995. UC Irvine statistician Jessica Utts, who uses statistical analysis and meta-analysis to study psi, and University of Oregon psychologist Ray Hyman, a noted psi skeptic, were commissioned by Congress and the CIA to evaluate the results of Stargate. They produced counterpoint reports in 1995: "An Assessment of the Evidence for Psychic Functioning" by Jessica Utts, "Evaluation of a Program on Anomalous Mental Phenomena" by Ray Hyman, and "Response to Ray Hyman's Report of September 11, 1995" by Jessica Utts, which appear in full in both *Journal of Parapsychology*, 1995, Vol. 59, No. 4 and *Journal of Scientific Exploration*, 1996, Vol. 10, No. 1. The reports are further reprinted in *Journal of Parapsychology*, 2018, Vol. 82, Suppl. Utts' original report is rebutted by Hyman and she, in turn, responds to his rebuttal. For anyone interested in Stargate, I recommend this material as the "signal in the noise" amid a great deal of writing and debate on the matter.

was pioneered as an academic field of study by the remarkable research psychiatrist Ian Stevenson (1918–2007) who founded the Division of Perceptual Studies at the University of Virginia and whose efforts I plan to consider in the future. For five decades, the conservative researcher "traveled six continents, accumulating more than 2,500 cases of young children who recounted details of previous lives, which he meticulously verified with witnesses, hospital records, autopsy reports, death certificates, and photographs," eulogized the *Journal of Near-Death Studies* in Spring 2007.

* * *

One of the most important figures in psychical research died of heart failure in 1992 at the tragically young age of 46. I referenced him earlier. His name is Charles Honorton, known to friends as Chuck. He had struggled with lifelong health issues. Honorton's passing was a tremendous loss for the field. It was the near-equivalent to losing Einstein at the dawn of his relativity theories. It is critical to understand what Honorton accomplished. The self-taught researcher began corresponding with J.B. Rhine from his St. Paul, Minnesota, home at age 13 after he had consumed all of the books on parapsychology at his local library. The prodigy ventured on an internship to the Parapsychology Laboratory in Durham at age 15. Precocious, dogged, idealistic, and possessed of a razor-sharp intellect, Honorton began studying at the University of Minnesota but returned to Duke to work with Rhine. He never completed his degree, a point of contention between the newcomer and his mentor.* Indeed, J.B. seemed not to have fully recognized Honorton's virtuosity at the time. Honorton was interested in studying psi under conditions of hypnosis, an area that did not specifically interest J.B., and the younger man often felt put off from his planned experiments.

In the late 1960s and 70s, Honorton moved on to direct research into dreams and ESP at the innovative Division of Parapsychology and Psychophysics at Maimonides Medical Center in Brooklyn, New York.** Stemming from that period, Honorton proceeded to assemble possibly the most significant body of data we possess in the parapsychology field. It was through a long-running series of experiments designed with colleagues in the 1970s and 80s known as the *ganzfeld experiments.* Ganzfeld is German for whole or open field. Honorton had an instinct for the conditions under which ESP or telepathy—mind-to-mind communication—might be heightened, which formed the basis of his studies.

Honorton noted that the classic Rhine experiments were largely focused on subjects believed to have a predilection for ESP. This highlights a subtle divide within the culture of parapsychology. J.B. believed that ESP may be detectable throughout the human population but was readily testable through figures who possess innate abilities. He did not consider ESP something for which you could train or that was necessarily intrinsic to everyone.

---

* *The Enchanted Voyager: The Life of J.B. Rhine* by Denis Brian (Prentice-Hall, 1982)

** "Federal Grant Supports ESP Dream Research at Maimonides" by Gordon T. Thompson, *New York Times,* November 25, 1973

Rather, J.B. focused on what he considered naturally gifted individuals who made prime subjects. "What we were interested in," he wrote in his 1937 book *New Frontiers of the Mind*, "was not finding out whether everyone possesses extra-sensory perceptive powers, but first whether *anybody* does." J.B. estimated that about one in five subjects had it. His assignation with gifted individuals might be called the X-Men approach in tribute to historian of religions Jeffrey J. Kripal who has probed the connections between the superhero mythos and modern metaphysics.

Honorton took a different tack. He wondered if perhaps we do not need X-Men to test for ESP. He pondered whether psychical abilities are, in fact, general throughout the population—but perhaps the psychical signal, so to speak, gets jammed or the psyche's circuitry gets overloaded due to excessive stimuli in daily life. (And this was, of course, in the predigital era before handheld devices overwhelmed our attention.) Maybe our ancient ancestors were better able to "tune in" because there is so much frenetic activity and sensory overload in the modern era. Honorton pondered what it might reveal to test for ESP among subjects who are placed into conditions of relaxed, comfortable sensory deprivation. He ventured that you may be able to spike the ESP effect if you place a subject into sensory-deprived conditions without noise or bright light, e.g., seating the person in a comfortable recliner in a noise-proof, dimly lit room or chamber, fitted with eyeshades, and wearing headphones that emit white noise. (In the adjacent photograph, I am seated in a sensory deprivation tank of this kind during a 2019 visit to the Rhine Research Center.) These conditions induce the state I have previously described as hypnagogia, a kind of waking hypnosis. To recap, you enter into the hypnagogic state twice daily: just before you drift to sleep at night and just as you are coming to in the morning. It is a deeply relaxed, motionless state in which you might experience hallucinatory or morphing images, like the bending-clocks in a Salvador Dalí landscape, or you might experience aural hallucinations or tactile sensations of weightlessness or heavy limbs. You may experience bodily paralysis. Yet you remain functionally awake insofar as you are self-aware and are able to direct cognition.

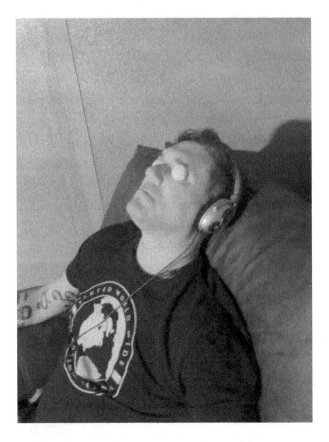

As explored in chapter nine, early twentieth-century French mind theorist Emile Coué, without the benefit of modern neuroscience and sleep studies (which have affirmed his instincts*) reasoned that this "in-between" state is prime time for reprogramming your subconscious through self-suggestion. He called the practice "conscious autosuggestion," which is basically self-hypnosis. For this, Coué prescribed his all-purpose mantra: *Day by day, in every way, I am getting better and better.* He said that you should gently whisper the mantra to yourself 20 times just before you drift to sleep at night and another 20 as you wake in the morning. The morning state is sometimes called hypnopompia (another term coined by psi research pioneer Frederic Myers). Hypnagogia and hypnopompia are similar with some differences, such as hallucinations occurring somewhat more commonly during the nighttime state.

Since hypnagogia is an apparently inviting period for self-suggestion—the mind is supple, the body relaxed, and the psyche unclouded by stimuli—Honorton pondered whether these conditions might facilitate heightened psychical activity. To test for telepathy, he placed one subject—called the receiver—into the relaxed conditions of sensory deprivation I have described, while a second subject—called the sender—is seated outside the sensory deprivation tank or in another space. In the classical ganzfeld experiments, the sender attempts to "transmit" a pre-selected image to the receiver. After the sending

---

* E.g., see "What Is the Link Between Hallucinations, Dreams, and Hypnagogic-Hypnopompic Experiences?" by Flavie Waters, et al., *Schizophrenia Bulletin*, 2016 Sept, 42(5), and "Neuro-hypnotism: prospects for hypnosis and neuroscience" by John F. Kihlstrom, *Cortex*, vol. 49, 2, 2013.

period ends, the receiver then chooses among four different images (one target image and three decoys) to identify what was sent.

Like the Zener cards, there is a randomly selected target on each successive trial and, in this case, a one-in-four or 25 percent chance of guessing right. In meta-analyzed data, subjects on average surpassed the 25 percent guess rate. Depending on the analytic model, the most stringently produced experiments demonstrated an overall hit rate of between 32 percent and 35 percent as examined in a 1994 meta-analysis.* Since the mid-1970s, this data has, in varying forms, been replicated by dozens of scientists across different labs in different nations, often under increasingly refined conditions. The ganzfeld experiments not only documented a significant psi effect but also suggested that a detectable ESP or telepathic effect may be more generally distributed among the population. The protocols themselves suggested conditions under which psi phenomena is most likely to appear.

Given its significance, the ganzfeld database attracted intense scrutiny. In a historic first, which has never really been repeated, Honorton in 1986 collaborated on a paper with a prominent psi skeptic, Ray Hyman, a professor of psychology at the University of Oregon. After trading written disputes over the validity of various parapsychological exper-

---

* "Does Psi Exist? Replicable Evidence for an Anomalous Process of Information Transfer" by Daryl J. Bem and Charles Honorton, *Psychological Bulletin*, 1994, Vol. 115, No. 1. Also see "Chapter 4: Experimental Research on Extrasensory Perception," *An Introduction to Parapsychology*, fifth edition by Irwin and Watt (McFarland, 2007): "In an assessment of the literature by Honorton (1978), 23 of 42 experiments conducted in ten different laboratories had yielded significant ESP performance under ganzfeld conditions; this success rate of 55% was far beyond that expected by chance."

iments and ganzfeld in particular, the interlocutors decided to collaborate on a joint study for the *Journal of Parapsychology*, analyzing the data, highlighting areas of agreement and dispute, and recommending protocols for future experiments. In an arena where arguments often devolve into ad infinitum rhetoric, it proved a signature moment.

"Instead of continuing with another round of our debate on the psi ganzfeld experiments," they wrote, "we decided to collaborate on a joint communiqué. The Honorton-Hyman debate emphasized the differences in our positions, many of these being technical in nature. But during a recent discussion, we realized that we possessed similar viewpoints on many issues concerning parapsychological research. This communiqué, then, emphasizes these points of agreement."*

Importantly—and in a statement that ought to serve as a general guardrail in our era of digital attack speech—they wrote: "Both critics and parapsychologists want parapsychological research to be conducted according to the best possible standards. The critic can contribute to this need only if his criticisms are informed, relevant, and responsible."

Beyond laying down general principles and research protocols, the collaborators conducted a joint meta-analysis of key ganzfeld experiments up to that moment. "The data base analyzed by Hyman and Honorton," wrote UC Irvine statistician Jessica Utts, "consisted of results taken from 34 reports written by a total of 47 authors. Honorton counted

---

* "A Joint Communiqué: The Psi Ganzfeld Controversy" by Ray Hyman and Charles Honorton, *Journal of Parapsychology*, vol. 50, December 1986

42 separate experiments described in the reports, of which 28 reported enough information to determine the number of direct hits achieved. Twenty-three of the studies (55%) were classified by Honorton as having achieved statistical significance at 0.05."* This figure, $P \leq 0.05$ (P=probability) is the commonly acknowledged bar of statistical significance within academic literature: your *null hypothesis*, or a lack of ESP effect in this case, has a less than 5 percent chance of being right. This success rate is similar to Honorton's findings in his 1978 meta-analysis.**

Notably, the psychical researcher and the skeptic wrote in their abstract: "We agree that there is an overall significant effect in this data base that cannot be reasonably explained by selective reporting or multiple analysis." And further within their paper: "Although we probably still differ on the magnitude of the biases contributed by multiple testing, retrospective experiments, and the file-drawer problem, we agree that the overall significance observed in these studies cannot reasonably be explained by these selective factors. Something beyond selective reporting or inflated significance levels seems to be producing the nonchance outcomes. Moreover, we agree that the significant outcomes have been produced by a number of different investigators." They went on:

> If a variety of parapsychologists and other investigators continue to obtain significant results under these

* "Replication and Meta-Analysis in Parapsychology" by Jessica Utts, *Statistical Science*, Vol. 6, No. 4, 1991

** See previous footnote of Irwin and Watt (McFarland, 2007).

conditions, then *the existence of a genuine communications anomaly will have been demonstrated.* [emphasis mine] The demonstration of an anomaly, of course does not explain it. Such a demonstration would, however, be very important because it would require acknowledgment that there is, indeed, something to be explained, and the debate would then shift toward such efforts. Whether the anomaly is ultimately to be considered "paranormal" will . . . depend on further developments such as the extent to which the findings can be brought under lawful control and the construction of a positive theory of the paranormal.

Hyman insisted that none of this was proof of psi, although he later allowed that "contemporary ganzfeld experiments display methodological and statistical sophistication well above previous parapsychological research. Despite better controls and careful use of statistical inference, the investigators seem to be getting significant results that do not appear to derive from the more obvious flaws of previous research."*

In sum, here was a key psychical researcher and a leading skeptic (Hyman was among the few skeptics who conducted his own research) disagreeing over the general nature of the ESP thesis—a reasonable disagreement—but affirming that the most important psychical data of the period proved unpolluted and that the methodology of the studies in their sample reflected significant improve-

---

* From Hyman's "Evaluation of a Program on Anomalous Mental Phenomena" (1995/1996) cited earlier.

ment from the dawn of the experiments in the early to mid 1970s (and warranted further refinement to which their paper was also dedicated). But the key data, they wrote, was free from substantial error, flaw, corruption, fraud, misinterpretation, mishap, or selective reporting. Hyman agreed that a statistically significant effect appeared in the data and justified further research. That's all. No concession of belief in ESP. Nor was any needed. Just an informed critique by a parapsychologist and a career-long skeptic, both with significant credentials, concluding that the data and practices were normative and a statistically significant anomaly appeared.

"To the best of our knowledge," Hyman and Honorton wrote, "this is the first time a parapsychologist and a critic have collaborated on a joint statement of this type." And further: "These propositions relate in general to how psi researchers and critics can work together toward the resolution of their differences."

It is tragic, both in terms of human pathos and intellectual advancement, that Honorton died six years after that paper was published. He was one of the only parapsychologists able to reach across the nearly unbridgeable partisan divide to a professional skeptic and create actual progress in terms of dialogue and research.* That process has never been repeated. Indeed, almost to the point of self-parody, as of this writing Wikipedia's article on the

---

* J.B. Rhine and his colleagues repeatedly made such efforts, even collaborating with overtly hostile critics, such as the originator of the aforementioned "trapdoor" thesis. More recently, parapsychologists including statistician Jessica Utts, biologist Rupert Sheldrake, and clinical psychologist Daryl J. Bem have also made such efforts with slender reciprocity.

ganzfeld experiments introduces them as a "pseudoscientific technique," without sourcing.

Most of the ESP debates are more a reflection of human nature than of actual intellectual dispute. But, still, it is worth asking why this chasm has remained so wide—and I will provide a recent case in point, if not to argue for my position, which is obviously favorable toward the ESP thesis, but to try and surmise, perhaps for myself personally, the facet of human nature that leads one to "flip over the chessboard" when a debate is not going your way.

*   *   *

Now, let me first note that, per the title of this chapter, wonderful strides have occurred in parapsychology. In fact, given the funding atmosphere, the advances are all the more impressive—but they are not what they could be. In referencing the 1995 cutoff of government funding for the Stargate Project—the CIA's "psychic spying" program got axed during post-Cold War budget cuts—a social sciences professor told me he was glad and that it was high time to "stop wasting the taxpayers' money."* During our debate, my interlocutor conceded the significance of the

---

* The rejectionist view is more widespread in the social sciences than in the natural sciences. As Cornell's Daryl J. Bem wrote in 2011 in the *Journal of Personality and Social Psychology*: "Psi is a controversial subject, and most academic psychologists do not believe that psi phenomena are likely to exist. A survey of 1,100 college professors in the United States found that psychologists were much more skeptical about the existence of psi than were their colleagues in the natural sciences, the other social sciences, or the humanities (Wagner & Monnet, 1979). In fact, 34% of the psychologists in the sample declared psi to be impossible, a view expressed by only 2% of all other respondents."

ganzfeld experiments but the following day reversed himself, leaving little point in further contention.

His comment referenced a popular misconception. In terms of calculable social factors, the call to arms—*stop wasting money!*—belies the reality of ESP research. In the same year as the Stargate cuts (the 20-year program cost about $20 million), statistician Jessica Utts, citing the work of psychologist Sybo Schouten, noted that during the more than 110 years since the founding of the Society for Psychical Research, "the total human and financial resources devoted to parapsychology since 1882 is at best equivalent to the expenditures devoted to fewer than two months of research in conventional psychology in the United States."* For comparison, the American Psychological Association reports that in 2017, $2 billion of the United States' $66.5 billion in federal research funding went to psychological research.** Think of it: the field of parapsychology has since its inception worldwide been funded in adjusted dollars at less than two months of traditional psychological experiments in the U.S. (experiments which, like much of the work in the social sciences, are overturned in routine cycles to reflect changes or corrections in methodology). That is less than $333,500,000, or a little more than the cost of four fighter jets. This figure compares with literally tens of trillions in adjusted dollars that have been spent worldwide during the same period on physics or medical research.

---

* From Utts' "Response to Ray Hyman's Report of September 11, 1995" cited earlier.

** "Federal research funding for psychology has not kept up with inflation" by Luona Lin, MPP, Peggy Christidis, PhD, and Jessica Conroy, BA, apa.org

This funding situation reflects, in part, the success of the most vociferous skeptics in disabling the legitimacy of parapsychological data, the capacity for serious dialogue between advocates and skeptics, and the professional and intellectual latitude granted researchers within the social and clinical sciences to work on questions of parapsychology. Most academic researchers steer clear, fearing damage to their reputation and ability to get other projects funded.

Even in this atmosphere, however, some scientists prevail against the tide. A historic episode occurred in 2011, which marked the publication of a paper called "Feeling the Future" by well-known research psychologist Daryl J. Bem of Cornell University. For about ten years, Bem conducted a series of nine experiments involving more than 1,000 participants into precognition or "time reversing" of widely established cognitive or psychological effects, such as memorization of a list or responding to negative or erotic stimuli flashed as images on a screen. Bem's discoveries demonstrated the capacity of cognition across boundaries of linear time.

Bem, as with other researchers including Dean Radin of IONS, identified factors that seem to correlate with precognition, such as the body's response to arousing or disturbing imagery. As Bem wrote of previous experiments in presentiment of stimuli: "Most of the pictures were emotionally neutral, but a highly arousing negative or erotic image was displayed on randomly selected trials. As expected, strong emotional arousal occurred when these images appeared on the screen, but the remarkable finding is that the increased arousal was observed to occur a few seconds before the picture appeared, before the computer had even selected the picture to be displayed." *

In one of Bem's trials, subjects were asked to "guess" at erotic images alternated with benign images. "Across all 100 sessions," he wrote, "participants correctly identified the future position of the erotic pictures significantly more frequently than the 50% hit rate expected by chance: 53.1% . . . In contrast, their hit rate on the nonerotic pictures did not differ significantly from chance: 49.8% . . . This was true across all types of nonerotic pictures: neutral pictures, 49.6%; negative pictures, 51.3%; positive pictures, 49.4%; and romantic but nonerotic pictures, 50.2%." ** The response to either arousing or disturbing imagery is suggestive of the *emotional stakes* required for the presence of a psi effect, to which J.B. Rhine alluded in the appendix to a British edition of his 1934 monograph *Extra-Sensory Perception:*

> Since my greatest interest is in stimulating others to repeat some of these experiments, I should like to mention here what has seemed to me to be the most important condition for ESP. This is *a spontaneity of interest in doing it.* The fresh interest in the act itself, like that of a child in playing a new game, seems to

---

* "Feeling the Future: Experimental Evidence for Anomalous Retroactive Influences on Cognition and Affect" by Daryl J. Bem, *Journal of Personality and Social Psychology,* 2011, Vol. 100, No. 3

** You will note the slender but statistically significant effect that is referenced here, which is typical of parapsychology experiments. The measurable impact is not like Zeus throwing lightning bolts at earth but rather a detectable "signal in the noise," which requires precise measurement and circumstantial cultivation.

me the most favorable circumstance. Add now . . . the freedom from distraction, the absence of disturbing skepticism, the feeling of confidence or, at least, of some hope, and I think many good subjects can be found in any community or circle.

This begins to suggest the bridge, however delicate, between parapsychology and the kinds of mind metaphysics explored in this book. In both categories, *passion is critical*. Stakes must exist and strong emotions must be in play, as explored in the previous chapter. In *New Frontiers of the Mind*, Rhine emphasized the role of spontaneity, confidence, comity, novelty, curiosity, and lack of fatigue. (And, as it happens, caffeine.)

But Bem's horizons extended further. In the most innovative element of his nine-part study, the researcher set out to discover in experiments eight and nine whether subjects displayed *improved recall* of lists of words that were to be practice-memorized *in the future*:

Inspired by the White Queen's claim, the current experiment tested the hypothesis that memory can "work both ways" by testing whether rehearsing a set of words makes them easier to recall—even if the rehearsal takes place after the recall test is given. Participants were first shown a set of words and given a free recall test of those words. They were then given a set of practice exercises on a randomly selected subset of those words. The psi hypothesis was that the practice exercises would retroactively facilitate the recall of those words, and, hence, participants would recall more of the to-be-practiced words than the unpracticed words.

Bem found a statistically significant improvement of recall on the lists of words studied in the near future: "The results show that practicing a set of words after the recall test does, in fact, reach back in time to facilitate the recall of those words." In experiment nine, this retroactive effect was heightened when researchers added a refined practice exercise. ("A new practice exercise was introduced immediately following the recall test in an attempt to further enhance the recall of the practice words. This exercise duplicated the original presentation of each word that participants saw prior to the recall test, but only the practice words were presented.") The results improved: "This modified replication yielded an even stronger psi effect than that in the original experiment." In general, future memorization heightened current recall.

Unsurprisingly, Bem's 2011 paper met with tremendous controversy. Some critics even suggested that his study was intended as satire or an exposé of foundational flaws in the scientific model of data gathering, although Bem's work in parapsychology had gone back many years. Abandoning earlier tones of probity, skeptic Ray Hyman told *The New York Times*: "It's craziness, pure craziness. I can't believe a major journal is allowing this work in. I think it's just an embarrassment for the entire field."* I have observed among psi skeptics a kind of reverse habit-

---

* "Journal's Paper on ESP Expected to Prompt Outrage" by Benedict Carey, *New York Times*, January 5, 2011

uation in matters of critical opinion. I have personally encountered skeptics, such as the Stargate funding critic referenced earlier, who in private or after extensive discussion will ease their tone of opposition, slacken their rejectionism, allow for intellectual exchange, and even acknowledge key data. But once they return to their peer groups, including on social media, they often revert to tones of unmitigated stridency.

Within a year of Bem's publication, a trio of professional skeptics published a rejoinder. Playing off of Bem's "Feeling the Future," their paper sported the media-friendly title, "Failing the Future."* The experimenters reran Bem's ninth experiment. They wrote in their abstract: "Nine recently reported parapsychological experiments appear to support the existence of precognition. We describe three pre-registered independent attempts to exactly replicate one of these experiments, 'retroactive facilitation of recall', which examines whether performance on a memory test can be influenced by a post-test exercise. All three replication attempts failed to produce significant effects . . . and thus do not support the existence of psychic ability."

You will recall that in his 1975 address to the Parapsychology Association Charles Honorton observed, "Even among parapsychologists there is a rather widespread belief that most of the independent replication of the early Duke work were non-confirmatory." I noted the confusion—some of it, I warrant, intentional—that

---

* "Failing the Future: Three Unsuccessful Attempts to Replicate Bem's 'Retroactive Facilitation of Recall' Effect" by Stuart J. Ritchie, Richard Wiseman, Christopher C. French, *PLoS ONE*, March 2012, Volume 7, Issue 3

polemical skeptics bring to this material in reference sources and media. This situation is so pronounced that on September 12, 2021, while writing this chapter, I privately emailed parapsychologist and friend Dean Radin: "Would you say that the Bem word-memory experiments are too pockmarked by data-gathering problems or lack of replicability to be ranked among core literature?" In his typically understated manner, Dean replied: "The Bem experiments are fine." This began my personal efforts to sort out what is unclear in dominant media and search rankings: the skeptics have cooked the books.

In the study that I cited above, "Failing the Future," the authors omitted a critical detail from their own database. By deadline, they possessed two independent studies that replicated Bem's results. They made no mention of the opposing studies despite their own ground rules for doing so. Bem wrote in his response:

In their article, [coauthor Stuart J.] Ritchie et al. mention that their experiments were "pre-registered." They are referring to an online registry set up by [coauthor Richard] Wiseman himself, asking anyone planning a replication to pre-register it and then to provide him with the data when the study is completed. As he noted on the registration website: "We will carry out a meta-analysis of all registered studies ... that have been completed by 1 December 2011."

By the deadline, six studies attempting to replicate the Retroactive Recall effect had been completed, including the three failed replications reported by Ritchie et al. and two other replications, both of which successfully reproduced my original findings at statistically significant levels. (One of them was conducted in Italy using Italian words as stimuli.) Even though both successful studies were pre-registered on Wiseman's registry and their results presumably known to Ritchie et al., they fail to mention them in this article.*

In the type of gear-grinding reply that renders these debates self-perpetuating and never-ending, the authors referenced *other studies* that had failed to reproduce Bem's results (at least one of them an online study that Bem disputed), without directly addressing his criticism.** The authors were scrupulous about this much: thanking Bem for making his database, software, and instructions available gratis to any researchers who wished to retread his efforts, which runs counter to the oft-heard canard that ESP experiments elude repetition or that parapsychologists avoid repeat trials.

In an otherwise caustic article written from the a priori assumption that ESP is impossible because it is impossible, journalist Daniel Engber noted in *Slate* in 2017: "To help get this project underway, Bem had granted researchers full access to his data and provided a detailed how-to guide for redoing his experiments—a level of transparency

---

* "Bem's response to Ritchie, Wiseman, and French," posted 15 Mar 2012: https://journals.plos.org/plosone/article/comment?id=10.1371/annotation/02eae6d6-af7f-41d8-b2b3-b6d32fdce7a6

** "Authors' response to Bem," posted 15 Mar 2012: https://journals.plos.org/plosone/article/comment?id=10.1371/annotation/cd8a1df4-e003-44aa-9d72-a7e1a6b26012

that was pretty much unheard of at the time."* Yet without considering the plausibility of psi beyond "it couldn't be true," in the words of a counter-researcher, the writer concluded: "Bem had shown that even a smart and rigorous scientist could cart himself to crazyland, just by following the rules of the road." Science itself is broken, the piece went, with Bem's analysis as exhibit A.

Although there unquestionably exists a significant crisis of replicability and data manipulation—not to mention fraud—in the social and natural sciences,** no one has directly tied any of this to Bem or his methods. Contrary to the stated nature of skepticism, however, inference sometimes trumps facts. On August 27, 2015, the *New York Times* ran an article, "Many Psychology Findings Not as Strong as Claimed, Study Says" by Benedict Carey. The piece dealt with a series of high-grade failures that rocked the social sciences over the previous several years, including misreports, research retractions, and fabrications. Amid this malfeasance, the opening paragraph read, "A top journal published a study supporting the existence of ESP that was widely criticized." It hyperlinked to Bem's study.

Bem's paper was grouped with, and cited as a prime exhibit of, polluted data. But not once in the article did

---

* "Daryl Bem Proved ESP Is Real: Which means science is broken" by Daniel Engber, *Slate*, June 7, 2017

** E.g., see "Why Most Published Research Findings Are False" by John P. A. Ioannidis, *PLoS Medicine*, August 2005, Volume 2, Issue 8. Much is sometimes made of the "decline effect" in Rhine's experiments—a topic that he addressed in detail and hypothesized over (e.g., see the previous statements from Rhine's *Extra-Sensory Perception* and *New Frontiers of the Mind*); this issue, too, is general to the medical and social sciences, e.g., "The Truth Wears Off: Is there something wrong with the scientific method?" by Jonah Lehrer, *The New Yorker*, December 5, 2010.

the reporter further reference Bem's study or support why it was categorized with fraudulent and compromised research. At the time, the paper maintained an editorial ombudsman. I wrote her to call this out. I received no reply. I wrote a letter to the editor. It did not run. I have written for the *New York Times* myself on controversial topics. A year before the article, I published an op-ed on the global problem of violence against accused witches.* In this case, however—with a controversial study coming from a respected researcher and published in a leading journal grouped *without explanation* with corrupted data—I could gain no evident hearing.

What about Bem's findings and the crisis of replication? I noted that Bem opened his database and software and provided instruction manuals free to anyone who wished to rerun his experiments. As of July 2020, Bem's experiments (including the original trials) showed replication in a meta-analysis encompassing 90 experiments in 33 laboratories in 14 countries.** Indulge my repetition of that figure. "To encourage replications," Bem and his coauthors wrote in the abstract of their follow-up paper, "all materials needed to conduct them were made available on request. We here report a meta-analysis of 90 experiments from 33 laboratories in 14 countries which yielded an overall effect . . . greatly exceeding" the standard

---

* "The Persecution of Witches, 21st-Century Style" by Mitch Horowitz, July 4, 2014

** "REVISED: Feeling the future: A meta-analysis of 90 experiments on the anomalous anticipation of random future events" [version 2; peer review: 2 approved] by Daryl Bem, Patrizio E. Tressoldi, Thomas Rabeyron, Michael Duggan, first published: 30 Oct 2015, latest published: 29 Jan 2016, last updated: 23 Jul 2020, *F1000Research*

for "'decisive evidence' in support of the experimental hypothesis."

I believe that I am highlighting only the glacial tip of how parapsychological data is mishandled within much of mainstream news media and large swaths of academia. The question is: *why?* I have difficulty understanding human nature, which is, finally, the crux of the matter. "The itch to silence those whose opinions we disagree with, applied centuries ago against scientists of the stature of Bruno, Galileo, and others, has spread, ironically, to scientists themselves, and there are few cases as blatant as those involving the topic of parapsychology," wrote Thorsen Professor of Psychology at Lund University, Sweden, Etzel Cardeña in 2015.* And further: "I think that a contributing factor is that research on parapsychology is seen as so emotionally (and factually) threatening because it suggests that 'things are not as they seem,' or at least as the censors believe they are."

Indeed, after a certain point of tautological criticism of nearly a century of academic ESP research, it becomes difficult to avoid using a strong word that I prefer not to use and that I do not use lightly: suppression. Not of any centrally organized sort but of a *cultural sort* in which prevailing findings run so counter to materialist assumptions that critics—who ironically perceive themselves as arbiters of rationality—assume an "at any cost" stance to dispel contrary data. Winning becomes more

---

* "The Unbearable Fear of Psi: On Scientific Suppression in the 21st Century," *Journal of Scientific Exploration*, Vol. 29, No. 4, December 15, 2015

important than proving. It is the antithesis of science. This is the irony to which professional skepticism has brought us.

*   *   *

I will offer a final illustration and then return to an important point about scientific understanding clashing with human nature. October of 2020 marked the death of the best-known critic of parapsychology, James Randi, a stage magician who had dedicated his career to exposing psychic fakery and what he considered the fallacies of parapsychology. Some of what Randi did was worthwhile. But my chief interest is in evaluating parapsychology as fairly as I am able—I am obviously favorable—and defending its findings where they deserve defending. In that vein, I published an article about Randi's career upon his death called "The Man Who Destroyed Skepticism." I was extremely critical. I had my reasons and I will reference just one.

During Randi's career, he maintained an educational foundation whose activities, as noted in my piece, were not always clear. But the James Randi Educational Foundation did issue a short guidebook for schoolteachers to teach students in grades 9 through 12 about ESP research and parapsychology, including the work of J.B. Rhine. As of this writing, it remains available online. *Do You Have ESP?: Teacher Edition* (which is copyrighted 2010 and 2012) states without sourcing: "It is now well established that Rhine and his colleagues had been allowing themselves to ignore much of the data they had collected and reported only those with positive results. Negative data were set aside."

I made the point earlier in this chapter that Rhine not only reported all results but, at a time when it was common practice among social scientists to report selectively, he took the lead in reversing that convention and elevating the general standards of the field. In the 1940 book *Extra-Sensory Perception After Sixty Years*, Rhine and his collaborators assembled all data, including that which remained unpublished. "From what is known at this stage of the research," they wrote, "odds appear to favor a tendency to suppress confirmatory results and to hasten to publish those which fail to confirm."

As noted, they meta-analyzed *everything* before that practice was common or the term coined. In a nearly remarkable exception, even Wikipedia, as of this writing, states in its article on "Meta-analysis:"

> The first meta-analysis of all conceptually identical experiments concerning a particular research issue, and conducted by independent researchers, has been identified as the 1940 book-length publication *Extrasensory Perception After Sixty Years*, authored by Duke University psychologists J. G. Pratt, J. B. Rhine, and associates. This encompassed a review of 145 reports on ESP experiments published from 1882 to 1939, and included an estimate of the influence of unpublished papers on the overall effect (the *file-drawer problem*).

Whatever one's perspective on the ESP thesis, this is the record.* Yet in a free guide, Randi overtly misled grade-school teachers into telling students that the problem with Rhine's research is *he hid bad results*. After decades in the media, the leading skeptic knew the facts.

As I have sought to demonstrate in this chapter, this kind of practice—in which self-perceived rationalists do injustice to truth in pursuit of what they consider a *defense of rationalism*—has run riot throughout the professional skeptics' field. I do not know where he finds the energy, but Cambridge biologist Rupert Sheldrake, in addition to his own research into psi phenomena, has proven determined and, in my estimate, intrepid in responding to serial problems among professional skeptics and the toll they have taken in reference media and journalism. I encourage exploration of his efforts.** Indeed, the level of invective currently directed against Sheldrake on Wikipedia is, in my view, warranting of that source's editorial supervision. In 2013, Sheldrake was named one of the top 100 Global Thought Leaders of the year by Switzerland's prestigious Duttweiler Institute. Today, on Wikipedia he is called a purveyor of "pseudoscience" for his theories of biological

---

* Rhine privately augmented this record when he wrote to mathematician Warren Weaver on March 15, 1960, in his aforementioned letter: "It is the rule, and it has always been the rule, to report every single test carried out with a subject for the experiment set up for his participation. By this I mean every single test carried out in the Laboratory under the conditions designed for the experiment."

** See www.sheldrake.org/reactions, which explores a variety of issues and offers resources that exceed my scope in this chapter. See also "Rationalists are wrong about telepathy" by Rupert Sheldrake, *Unherd*, Nov 22, 2021, and "Heads I Win, Tails You Lose" by Chris Carter, *Journal of the Society for Psychical Research* 74, 2010.

resonance and psi. Anyone who believes that researchers enter parapsychology with anything less than intellectual and personal fibrousness is unaware of the nature of the field. In that vein, I am reminded of the Emerson quote that appears in the book's introduction: "If Knowledge be power, it is also Pain."

*   *   *

I am dogged in criticizing the critics—what about the parapsychologists themselves? Is there fraud today in parapsychology, as in other sciences? And might that cancel out its statistical effects? This is, I believe, the line of reasoning that responsible skeptics ought to be pursuing rather than cooking data or the historical record to suit their tastes or engaging in the absurd denialism that exceptions to common observation are nullifying (which would have stopped the field of quantum physics in its tracks in the 1930s).

In 2015, Douglas M. Stokes, a mathematical psychologist and former associate editor of the *Journal of Parapsychology*, laid out the case that the statistical significance for psi phenomena could be wiped out by levels of fraud in the field commensurate to or lower than those found in other branches of the sciences.* I mentioned earlier that the social and natural sciences are experiencing a credibility gap, which may be a longstanding issue now coming to light due to increased scrutiny. Based on cur-

---

* "The Case Against Psi" by Douglas M. Stokes, *Parapsychology: A Handbook for the 21st Century* edited by Etzel Cardeña, John Palmer and David Marcusson-Clavertz (McFarland, 2015)

rent analysis and surveys, Stokes wrote that fraud rates in biomedical and psychology research are probably at a respective 9 percent and 10 percent. As a result, additional studies suggest that "the use of the traditional 0.05 level of statistical significance as the criterion for the admission of a research finding into the academic literature will result in a majority of the published findings being false, once false positives are taken into account." Based on Stokes's modeling, if overall fraud rates in parapsychology are just under half of those in other sciences, the deception would prove significant enough to eliminate statistical proof in favor of the null hypothesis.

It is easy to assume the persistence of fraud in parapsychology. After all, the Society for Psychical Research began in 1882 with the express purpose of rooting out fraud among mediums (who should not, of course, be conflated with parapsychologists) and bringing greater standards to assertions of extra-physicality. In the early 1970s, J.B. Rhine's then-independent lab (faced with declining institutional support his center had migrated off campus) was itself rocked by a fraud scandal. A charismatic and driven medical student handpicked by Rhine as his institutional successor was caught faking results. Rhine was resolute and transparent in rooting out and exposing the fraud and laying groundwork for improvements.[*]

But Rhine cannot wholly be spared blame. He handpicked his own Judas. "He had barely been there three

---

[*] See "A new case of experimenter unreliability" by J.B. Rhine, *Journal of Parapsychology*, 38, 1974, and "Comments: A second report on a case of experimenter fraud," *Journal of Parapsychology*, 39, 1975.

years," wrote authorized biographer Denis Brian, "when, in 1973, Rhine appointed this man in his early twenties director of the institute."* It is possible that Rhine, a former Marine with square-jawed good looks and poised manners, saw in this "bright young dynamo" a formidable newcomer who could take parapsychology to its next stage of public acceptance. From my perspective, it would have been wiser for Rhine to place his stock in the less-Olympian looking but more integral and erudite Charles Honorton with whom Rhine never seemed to personally connect. Although Honorton's career was cut short by ill-health, the scientist proved the field's natural intellectual heir, but without the garland of institutional inheritance.

For all that, I consider it fair to state that parapsychology today may be among the *few exceptions* to common fraud in the social sciences. When I posted about the matter in late 2021 on social media, parapsychology journalist Craig Weiler put it this way:

> Because parapsychology doesn't convey any honors from successful research, either through social acknowledgment or an improvement in professional status, there is little motivation for cheating. Successful studies also have to run the skeptical gauntlet. So, little incentive … Just a personal observation, the field seems to attract uncorruptible people. The people who take it seriously and publicly, have to have a generally reduced fear level and be willing to fight for

---

* *The Enchanted Voyager: The Life of J.B. Rhine* (Prentice-Hall, 1982)

the importance of truth. That doesn't describe your average cheater.*

In any case, I celebrate Stokes as an informed parapsychological researcher (he spent twenty years reviewing results for the *Journal of Parapsychology*) to take a position of tough-minded heterodoxy. Indeed, it is infinitely more important to me as an advocate of parapsychology research—and it would epitomize the worst kind of intellectual politics to try to conceal that—that we *get it right* versus win a debate. I would rather lose ground a hundred times over than proffer an argument that is strictly rhetorical or tactical in nature or that misrepresents key findings when a debate goes against me. That is why I am so flummoxed, perhaps naively, when I encounter skeptics—and skeptic is a noble title that any of us should be glad to claim—who use deceptive or slippery methods in the interest of promulgating intellectual soundness. If that makes me naïve, it is another appellation that I wear proudly.

*   *   *

Once again: the point is not to win but to search. To honor the basic human question of what lies around the next hill. Our society needs greater academic and intellectual leeway in this area so that parapsychologists need not fear damage to career or reputation. As noted, psi research is inexpensive. Because the skeptics have proven so success-

---

* Weiler's book *Psi Wars* (White Crow Books, 2013/2020) is an important (and unsettling) overview of the current crisis of skepticism, including how the tech-boosterish TED Talks have silenced parapsychologists.

ful, however, most parapsychologists today must secure independent funding. Anyone who has written grant proposals knows that that process can be the equivalent of a job in itself. But the men and women who populate parapsychology today carry out this labor while also conducting their research and often holding academic or clinical positions to pay the bills. What's more, they often endure professional insults and sometimes suffer calumny. Simply put, they are the punks of the scientific world—and they have the scars to prove it.

In terms of background, lifestyle, and social-political outlook, I probably differ little from most critics of parapsychology. I recognize that skeptics fear a wave of irrationality will be unleashed on the world if headlines start announcing, "Harvard Study Says ESP Is Real"—they strive against that day (although in various forms it has already come and gone). In the aforementioned exchanges with Freud, his long-suffering biographer Ernest Jones protested that acknowledging telepathy "would mean admitting the essential claim of the occultists that mental processes can be independent of the human body."*

My contention is that seriousness derives not from the nature of your query or associations but from your

---

* Freud himself appeared more sanguine on the matter, responding: *"Dans ces cas pareils, ce n'est que le premier pas qui coute. Das weistere findet sich"*—"It is only the first step that counts. The rest follows." On July 24, 1921, Freud wrote even more bluntly to British-American psychical researcher, Hereward Carrington: "I do not belong with those who reject in advance the study of so-called occult phenomena as being unscientific, or unworthy, or harmful. If I were at the beginning of my scientific career, instead of at the end of it as I am now, might perhaps choose no other field of study—in spite of all its difficulties." For this reference, I am indebted to Raymond Van Over, "Freud and Occultism," letter, *New York Times*, May 19, 1974.

demonstrable tools and excellence. This does not devolve into license to "ask anything." Queries intended to deny the humanity of another or that fly in the face of well-documented public safety (such as the benefits of vaccines and seatbelts) or overwhelming soundness of record (like the moon landing) corrode our culture and common well-being. My wish is simply to see parapsychological inquiry carried out unhindered by false criticism and untethered from polemically driven funding droughts.

The issues I am describing have easily cost us more than a generation of progress in parapsychology. We are at least 30 or 40 years behind where we ought to be, dated from when the professional skeptical apparatus began to ramp-up in the mid-1970s. One of the real challenges for parapsychology—and addressing this is, I think, necessary to the field's next leap forward—is to arrive at a *theory of conveyance.* I believe the field needs a persuasive theoretical model that pulls together the effects and posits how information is transferred in a manner unbound by time, space, distance, linearity, and common sensory experience. Researchers have made preliminary steps in this direction.* Advances are overdue.**

---

* E.g., a partial overview appears at the Global Consciousness Project: https://noosphere.princeton.edu/speculations.html. For a fuller perspective on theories of psi and related issues, the motivated student will feast upon the two-volume set, *Extrasensory Perception: Support, Skepticism, and Science* edited by Edwin C. May and Sonali Bhatt Marwaha (Praeger, 2015).

** It is also worth noting the social barriers to this undertaking. Scientist Dean Radin remarked to me on December 29, 2021, that arriving at a theory of psi "will almost certainly require a radical change to the current mainstream worldview, and pushing against the inertia of that status quo is, to put it mildly, not so simple because of the sociopolitical reasons you've already alluded to. Prominent people's careers and legacies are at stake."

*   *   *

Earlier I mentioned J.B. Rhine's exchange of letters with mathematician Warren Weaver, a highly regarded mathematical engineer and grant-making science foundation executive. Speaking of Rhine's methodology, which he had studied, Weaver in 1960 uttered a semi-famous lament about ESP research at a panel discussion at Dartmouth College: "I find this whole field [parapsychology] intellectually a very painful one. And I find it painful essentially for the following reasons: I cannot reject the evidence and I cannot accept the conclusions."* Weaver caught hell for his statement; some colleagues questioned whether his judgment had slipped; a few others (including Dartmouth's president) privately thanked him for broaching the topic.

Weaver had toured Rhine's labs in early 1960. On February 22, he privately wrote Rhine to raise several issues. Near the top of his seven-page, singled-spaced letter, Weaver made this point: "For if you could make substantial progress in analyzing, explaining, and controlling, then the problem of *acceptance* would be largely solved."** Rhine had long labored to demonstrate *effect*, Weaver wrote, but he now needed to describe *mechanics*. His letter continued:

---

* For Weaver's statement and its background, see *Unbelievable* by Stacy Horn (HarperCollins/Ecco, 2009).

** Weaver's letter and Rhine's reply are from the Parapsychology Laboratory Records, 1893–1984, Rare Book, Manuscript, and Special Collections Library, Duke University, Durham, NC.

But for three main reasons—or at least so it seems to me—the problem of acceptance remains. First, these phenomena are so strange, so outside the normal framework of scientific understanding, that they are inherently very difficult to accept. Second, the attempts to analyze, understand, and control have not been, as yet, very successful or convincing. And third, unreasonable and stubborn as it doubtless appears to you, very many scientists are not convinced by the evidence which you consider is more than sufficient to establish the reality of the psi phenomena.

Rhine replied on March 15 in general agreement with Weaver's framing:

... the three main reasons you give in your analysis are recognizably correct. Had you been inclined at this point to go a step further into the intellectual background for these reasons, this might have been the point to draw upon the judgments of some of the philosophers and other commentators who have dealt with the problem of acceptance. There is an increasingly candid recognition of the difficulty as an essentially metaphysical one. Psi phenomena appear to challenge the assumption of a physicalistic universe.

I have made it clear that Rhine is an intellectual hero to me. Yet I detect in his response an effort to sidestep Weaver's challenge. Rhine acknowledges the difficulty of acceptance; but rather than take up the question of mechanics, he ascribes Weaver's concern to the field of social or metaphysical philosophy. That, at least, is my reading. I talked this over with Rhine's eldest daughter, Sally Rhine Feather, a clinical psychologist who past the age of 90 remains active with the center her parents founded.

On September 20, 2021, I wrote Sally: "I am wondering whether J.B. ever privately pondered, or wrote down, a theorized delivery mechanism for ESP?" She graciously replied the same day:

> I have never known him to have gone very far in this direction—sadly, J.B. never got to the memoirs he should have written before his health declined in his last year. But he was always so cautious at going beyond the data and had this aversion to philosophers who did so—except for the implications of the non-physical nature of psi on which he actually speculated extremely broadly at times. Best I have are some general clues. When I asked him about being a dualist or a monist, when I was a young person he gave me the analogy of looking at a pair of trousers from the bottom up, and somehow there would be a common force or energy, that would make him only a relative dualist ... And there are many quotes of a grander nature (in *New World of the Mind*) that suggest—"It will be the task of biophysics and psychophysics to find out if there are unknown, imperceptible, extraphysical influences in nature that function in life and mind, influences which can interact with detectable physical processes ..."

Hence, Rhine saw his research mission as shaping protocols to obtain and analyze reliable evidence—not venturing a theory of mechanics. (Rhine also noted that evidence for ESP—for the mind liberated from "the cardinal properties of matter, space, and time"—was a necessary prerequisite to considering the after-death survival thesis.*) In his response to Weaver, Rhine was, of course, referencing commonly accepted physical laws at the time. For psychical researchers today, studies in quantum theory, retrocausality, extra-dimensionality, neuroplasticity, string theory, and "morphic fields" that enable communication at the cellular level (the innovation of Rupert Sheldrake) suggest a set of physical laws that surpass the known and that may serve as a kind of "macroverse" within which familiar mechanics are experienced. It was already clear in Rhine's era that extrasensory transmission could not be explained through the "mental radio" model, since, according to Rhine's tests and those of others, ESP is unaffected by time, distance, or physical barriers. This rebounds the question: If the psi effect is real, *how does it work*? How does mentality exceed the obvious boundaries of sensory transmission?

Perhaps science overvalues theory. In a talk that novelist Michael Crichton had hoped to deliver to ESP rejectionists at Caltech (but he got ghosted after a preliminary invitation was floated), the writer observed:

The problem of data in conflict with existing theory cannot be overstated. Arthur Eddington once

---

* Mauskopf and McVaugh (1980)

said you should never believe any experiment until it has been confirmed by theory, but this humorous view has a reality that cannot be discounted . . . data to support the idea of evolution—such as the fossil record—were long known; but a convincing theory to explain the data was lacking. Once Darwin provided the theory, the data were accepted.*

Crichton compared this to the common skeptics' claim that there exists no evidence at all for ESP. I have personally encountered mentalists (magicians who perform as psychics), social scientists, physicians, editors, novelists, and journalists—some thoughtful and gifted, others churlish and lazy—who state confidently that there is not a "shred of evidence" for ESP (a stock phrase that psi researchers sometimes joke over). Is the absence of theory blinding our intellectual culture to the evidence? And does this blinkered vision finally matter? The public tends toward sympathy of ESP—not something I consider a valid measure of truth, but worth noting. Crichton further quoted Nobel Prize winner in physics Max Planck: "A new scientific truth does not triumph by convincing its opponents and making them see the light, but rather because its opponents eventually die, and a new generation grows up that is familiar with it." This may be the position in which orthodox materialists find themselves today.

Nonetheless, I believe that it falls to each generational cohort to venture a theory of phenomena in which it pro-

---

* "Postscript: Skeptics at Cal Tech," *Travels* by Michael Crichton (Knopf, 1988)

fesses deep interest. That theory can ignite a debate—it can be thrown out and replaced, it can be modified—but I do not believe that researchers and motivated lay inquirers (like me) can eschew the task. For this reason, I attempted a theory of mind causation in the closing chapter of my 2018 book *The Miracle Club* entitled, "Why It Works."

Consider this: when you say the word *precognition* it strikes many people as fantastical, as though we are entering crystal-ball territory. I do not believe in altering vocabulary to suit reactions (or that it does any good). But why the incredulity? We already know, and have known for generations, that *linear time as we experience it is an illusion*. Einstein's theories of relativity, and experiments that have affirmed them, establish that time slows in conditions of extreme velocity—at or approaching light-speed—and in conditions of extreme gravity like a black hole. The individual traveling in a metaphorical space-ship at or near lightspeed experiences time slowing (not from their perspective but in comparison to those not at near lightspeed), and this is not a mere thought exercise.* Space travelers in our era, although they are obviously not approaching anywhere near that velocity, experience minute effects of time reduction.**

In short, linear time is a *necessary illusion* for five-sensory beings to get through life. Time is not an absolute. What's more, I hope that we as a culture are coming to

---

* Einstein famously wrote in a letter of March 1955, "People like us, who believe in physics, know that the distinction between past, present, and future is only a stubbornly persistent illusion."

** E.g., see "Here's why astronauts age slower than the rest of us here on Earth" by Kelly Dickerson, *Business Insider*, August 19, 2005.

a greater understanding of interdimensionality through models like string theory—which, it must be noted, are not reality but suppositions of reality—and are learning further about the infinitude of objects and events, such as we glean from quantum physics and experiments that branch off from them. We may further come to realize, as noted earlier, that our senses are organic devices used to *measure things*. What else are sight, hearing, taste, touch, and sound? In the particle lab, researchers use finely tuned instruments to measure infinitesimally small objects. These subatomic particles appear in so-called superposition or a wave state until a measurement is made either by a sentient observer or an automatic device, thus collapsing a particle from a possibility to an actual event. (This wave state is not limited to small objects alone but is seen, for example, in liquid helium reduced to temperatures of near zero.*) Moreover, the decision to take or not take a measurement at a given moment determines not only what we will experience locally but, it stands to reason, *an infinitude of concurrent realities*, or "many worlds" in the interpretation of physicist Hugh Everett III, which are set into motion—in an actual genesis of selection—based on when or whether you elect to measure. We face an infinitude of concurrent realities—not in possibility but in actuality—one of which we will localize or experience within our framework based upon perspective or when we look. Those interpretations emerge from 90 years of quantum physics experiments.

---

* See the extraordinary BBC video: https://www.youtube.com/watch?v=9FudzqfpLLs

To switch tacks, in the field known as string theory, we encounter a theoretical model that seeks to explain some of the surrealism detected not only within particle mechanics but also within standard Newtonian mechanics, such as how both micro and macro objects at vast distances have been observed to mirror one another. String theory posits that all of reality is interconnected by vast networks of vibrating strings. Everything from the tiniest particle to entire universes to other dimensions are linked by these undulating strings. Hence, something that occurs within another dimension not only affects what happens in the reality of the dimension that we occupy but signals an infinitude of events playing out in these other fields of existence, as in ours.

We may even crisscross into these concurrent realities, hence conducting lives that are infinite in terms of the psyche and variable in dimensional occupancy, as considered in chapter five, "Time Travel." Experiencing data or events from other dimensions may also be extrapolated to UFO encounters or other anomalous phenomena, something considered in my chapter "Reclaiming the Damned" in the anthology *Uncertain Places*. Within current theoretical structures, it is actually *easier* to understand UFOs as interdimensional rather than interstellar since interstellar travel is more difficult to fathom according to existing models of velocity (e.g., Einstein's special relativity), which place an upper limit on how fast an object can travel through ordinary space.*

---

* I should also note that the theory of wormholes—or "tunnels" through ordinary spacetime—might explain how one could travel around the universe very quickly without violating lightspeed. This does not necessarily mean going into or through other dimensions of reality.

Perhaps an individual, either because he or she is uniquely sensitive at a given moment or experiences a reduction of sensory data while retaining awareness, as in the ganzfeld experiments, is capable of accessing information—or taking measurements—from other states or dimensions that exist along the theorized bands of strings. We call these measurements precognition, telepathy, ESP, or psychokinesis, the last of which may be a form of pre-awareness or movement or both.* But perhaps that is simply *what finer measurement looks like.* It is possible that measurement not only informs but also, or at least in certain cases, actualizes, localizes, and determines. *Measurement selects.* That is the contention of this book.

As observed, a law in order to be such, must be consistent. If there is a law of extrasensory perception, that law may be constant but also experienced unevenly based on surrounding circumstances, as with other natural laws. We may get distracted, overloaded, fatigued, and attenuated to experiencing reality. This may be our general state. ESP is bound up with other factors. "And so ESP, whatever it may be," J.B. Rhine wrote in *New Frontiers of the Mind*, "is at any rate a part of the general complex process-system that we call the mind, or to be still more inclusive, of the personality as a whole." Perhaps if we gleaned what

---

* "A definite relation between ESP and PK is suggested," the Rhines wrote in their 1943 paper on psychokinesis, "one in which each complements the other much as in the analogous relation between sensory perception and motor abilities . . ." Indeed, this highlights the difficulty of arriving at a theory: "Not only is a persuasive theoretical explanation for precognition unavailable at this point," wrote Julia Mossbridge and Dean Radin in their previously cited 2018 paper, "but we do not even know whether we should be attempting to identify one mechanism or many."

was actually going on, or exercised fuller capacities of sensation, the experience would prove overwhelming. We would be overcome with data. Hence, we may *need* a linear sense of time and a limited field of information in order to *navigate experience.*

And yet: given that we understand spacetime as flexible, is it really so strange, so violative of our current body of knowledge, that there exist *quantifiable exceptions to ordinary sensory experience*? As we document these exceptions, trace their arc, and replicate the conditions under which they occur, perhaps we approach what poet and mystic William Blake foresaw in 1790 in *The Marriage of Heaven and Hell*: "If the doors of perception were cleansed every thing would appear to man as it is: Infinite." And thus ineffable.

Postscript

On my left forearm is a tattoo reading, "A is A." It is an Aristotelian formula adapted by the radical individualist philosopher Ayn Rand affirming, chin out, that objective truth exists and is deducible. It represents one facet of my metaphysics, on display throughout much of this chapter.

But there is another facet, as well.

There are limits to the degree to which the ineffable can be captured in a laboratory setting. As historian of religions Jeffrey J. Kripal—my own Professor X—wrote me in early 2022, "The notion that 'passion is critical' is embedded in the coinage of the term 'telepathy' or 'pathos at a distance' and not 'indifferent neutrality at a distance.' [F.W.H.] Myers, in fact, linked telepathy to eros."

And further, "My general sense . . . is that the para-psychological evidence is still statistical, and that the best evidence is experiential or spontaneous, as the Rhines knew well. I think the scientific method is a perfect method to make the psi effect go away or disappear. It's like going to the North Pole to find zebras. The actual going there makes seeing zebras impossible."

The ineffable is necessarily intimate, uneven, and sometimes—often outside the electrode, clipboard atmosphere of a lab—shattering and extraordinary, such as in moments of crisis when someone foresees a loved one in danger.

During my years in book publishing, I encountered some writers who faked stuff. Even made up Nostradamus quatrains. It chafed against everything in me. That is one of the many reasons why the squared-jawed, ethical J.B. Rhine has been such an influence on me. But I recognize the truth of Jeff's points, which he explores in his many books, including *Authors of the Impossible*. Indeed, we have already gathered so much clinical evidence for ESP that it overflows the archives. (This is, in some cases, literally so.) Continuing to pursue the truth in such a situation can be, as philosopher Jacob Needleman once alluded, "like having the *nicest* cell in the prison." We cannot keep accumulating empiricism according to nineteenth-century models and saying that we have attained truth—although it *is* truth—while doing battle with ears-plugged, eyes-closed skeptics.

Years ago, I talked some of this over with parapsychologist Lawrence LeShan, who died at age 100 on November 9, 2020. He had spent a considerable part of his career studying the psychical within the strict empirical model and he was attempting to articulate something like the points that I quoted from Jeff Kripal.

Lawrence was elderly at the time, not in the best health (we had to order in food at his apartment on Manhattan's Upper West Side because getting around was sometimes difficult for him), and he was struggling, not in a negative way, to get across to me that after years of compiling stats and documenting the paranormal in clinical settings, he believed that the field needed to go in a different direction; that everything that could be "proven" within the current paradigm already had been. He noted in *A New Science of the Paranormal* in 2009: "Stop trying to prove the existence of psi and get on with studying its properties. If someone does not believe the proofs already published, he or she is not going to believe new ones."

Of course, there are important new experiments—including Bem's precognition work—that open fresh and extraordinary windows. Perhaps we must gaze back to the value that William James placed on individual experience, testimony, and empiricism—and gaze forward to the value that Jeff Kripal places on revelation, the determinative nature of belief (all beliefs), and the harmonizing complex of story—to finally understand what paranormalist writer Charles Fort called our "wild talents."

We need both the data table and the moonlit night. We are creatures of both.

The Bird-Lizard
a true story

Tonight, I paddled my kayak across a lake in upstate New York. It was well after dark.

As I approached the eastern shoreline, I spotted the shadowy outline of a creature, no larger than an ibis, walking along the water's edge.

At first, I was sure it was a waterbird, but as I gazed at it more carefully, I detected the shape and movements of a lizard.

I thought about turning on my flashlight, but it seemed out of keeping with the moment.

I began to feel the sense that there was something instructive about this experience.

"May I ask you a question?" I asked the bird-lizard.

I got no response.

"Do you have a message for me?"

Still, no response.

But then I realized: The message was in the creature's movements.

It moved deftly. But without fear.

Chapter Thirteen

What Do You Want?

What do you wish for at this instant?

Be stark. Recall the power of a wish described earlier.

The sense of selfhood contained within a wish—the direction in which you desire to move, the expression you yearn to enact—is profoundly private. It is your own. It is meaningful to you on terms that you as a mature person need never justify to another.

In that vein, I ask you to think very carefully of what you truly wish for in life. This wish should never be a source of embarrassment. Because, if sincere, it may arise from a place of deep need. It may signal the environment, settings, circumstances, or people among which you feel *most natural*.

It may help if you think about the nature of your earliest fantasies, what you wished for at the youngest age from which you retain memories. Perhaps age three or four, when you first began to form recallable, long-term memories and self-conscious cognition. We obviously possess infantile emotional memories but these are not always easily summoned. Your earliest fantasies, dreams, and wishes are precious because they occurred prior to the calcification of peer pressure, which eventually shapes and colors our internal voices and even most intimate self-perceptions. Probably by the time a child reaches age nine, he or she is locked into the gravitational conditioning of peer pressure. Hence, the things that we repeat within assume a rote and recitative quality. How much of who we believe ourselves to be, or the measure we take of ourselves and our wishes, is internalized peer pressure? We often feel driven to affirm things that we believe make us look good to others, even as these dialogues occur within the confines of our psyches.

Catch a glimpse of yourself prior to that internalization. This is a practical book. Hence, I ask you this very night, perhaps just before drifting to sleep, to allow yourself to return to those earliest memories. I believe that you will find within them something of your core being. And then return to the present and ask yourself whether—in the ways we have been considering—you are moving in the direction of your wishes. If you are, I would venture that you have probably experienced some encouragement and affirming signs, along with difficulty. And if you find that you are not, if you feel adrift, it may be that moving in that direction is the very thing that you have been looking for, not only for a sense of purpose but also because the *striving itself*, the focus itself, enacts selective, causative agencies.

As noted, I eschew the terms "attraction" or "manifestation." I do not find them sufficiently descriptive of what is occurring. They do not account for countervailing events or organic limits. Rather, I speak in terms of measurement and selection. You as an autonomous psyche possess capacities for measurement and selection—*use them.*

Passion is the vital component—probably the single greatest component of enacting the metaphysical processes of the psyche. This is why your wish, if it is to trigger these energies, must be absolutely authentic and real. I can think of few things more draining of your psychical capacities than having a wish taken away from you. Yet that is what many of our traditions and even our therapeutic culture sometimes does. We are told to redirect our wishes toward something more altruistic, communal, service oriented, practical, or immaterial. We comply—fitfully. We rework our wishes, at least in spoken or written word, into formulas for "making the world a better place." But we never feel entirely honest or self-integral when doing so. We blunt our passions.

One of the things I have discovered in parapsychology research is that results are most likely to appear in conditions of driven intensity, passion, and arousal, defined broadly. That fact has emerged from the experiments of J.B. Rhine from the early 1930s to Daryl J. Bem in the second decade of the twenty-first century.

I believe that *ardent desire* can activate the energies of causation as much as *imagined fulfillment.* And the former step may meet you more on your own terms. We can always *feel* a real wish. Because natural mechanics are conditioned by circumstance, however, we may not be able to select the precise nature of *how* a wish is fulfilled. Our powers may be limited to select circumstance and not specifics. (Although sometimes we get exactly what we want—like pink buckets.) The arrival of the situation or thing will likely occur through available mechanisms. Indeed, what reaches you through such mechanisms may, if recognized, prove better suited to you or more appropriate than what you have pictured. In general, I do not believe that we select things; I believe that we select *circumstance*, which is mitigated by and interwoven with surrounding conditions and realities. Circumstance can reach us in wild, unexpected, and even unsettling ways. It can also require payment in commensurate kind, a subtle law of life.

Sometimes payment is made in the form of what might be called *ersatz deliverance*. This occurs when you think you have received what you wanted but it turns out to be false gold. For example, you may enter the wrong relationship, job, or business partnership—it is the thing that you think you "selected" but it goes quickly awry or does not finally pan out. The real thing does not arrive until later. This has happened to me in relationships. Someone who I thought was just right proved unavailable or wholly wrong, only to be followed, sometimes months later, by the right person. This has happened to me, too, in business relations.

There may be several reasons why we experience ersatz deliverance. As noted, the desired thing must reach us through *established channels*. That is, byways and economies of the human situation that already exist. Nature operates by its most efficient means. It will not produce a thing *that is not*, so much as employ resources and circumstances *that are*. You will not find water in the desert without an arduous and energy-sapping search. Water will readily appear in fertile regions. Ask yourself what people and situations reflect those terrains in your life. If a person or a collective institution—institutions have a culture and psychology of their own—does not see or "get" you, chances are you need to replant your efforts elsewhere. Indeed, it is possible that your life does not yet have the connections, channels, and circuitry for what you need. Hence, what appears is not the desired condition, person, or object but an incomplete variant of it. I do not mean to sound a note of limit; I have spoken of interdimensional selection. But still, we must sometimes contend with remnants, legacies, and elements attached to our lives, however broadly or even infinitely conceived. It is also possible that you may not possess the skill or psychology to manage the wished-for thing. Training wheels may be required. Self-lessons, sometimes tough in nature, may be needed.

At times, you may find it helpful to conceive of your own form of payment. I wrote in chapter three that "there is a price paid and good received for everything and this exchange cannot be abrogated." For example, I struggle with smoking. I give myself permission to be a "social smoker" but the habit usually escalates from there. Recent to this writing, I gave up smoking (or tried to)—I sacrificed it to my deity—in exchange for something I wanted, to which I allude in the next section. The concept of sacrifice or payment, as a meaningful form of reciprocal exchange, is something to consider.

* * *

From the perspective of philosophical pragmatism and the search, the only question that matters is: does it work? Hence, I have determined to close this book by providing you with a simple formula composed of: 1) focused desire; 2) enunciation; 3) sex transmutation; and 4) acceptance of channels. I will walk you through each step, as I practiced it in real time while writing this chapter.

Focused Desire

I am going to be extremely, even uncomfortably, blunt with you. If I am not transparent, I am sidestepping. I am evading. Cynics see transparency as self-absorption. That is their own projection. Transparency is idealism. Because it requires the subject to stand bare in service of exploring pragmatic philosophy, to which this book is dedicated.

My focused, impassioned desire was fame. Not of some cheap, gaudy sort, and not as an "influencer" (which is an advertising term), but rather fame in a classical sense: receiving honorable recognition for achievement. I will not apologize for or equivocate over that point. I trust the mature individual to clarify and progress toward his or her private sense of meaning. We know more than we think we do about ourselves and our authentic needs. The sensitive individual is often wiser than thought habits codified across generations and recited back as traditions.

Familiarity is not truth. Passion is. It cannot be concealed or sublimated—for long.

Enunciation

Clarity is critical. An author once maintained to me the importance of distilling your aim to a single word, as I have just done. At first, that approach sounded unrealistically narrow. I thought I understood focus. But, in actuality, there is one element of your aim that stands out above all the others. For example, money matters to me—but it is secondary to fame, as I have defined it. Often, your prime objective serves as a pathway to filling myriad needs (including those of others), but your most driving factor is what really matters to us here.

This selection can be a challenge. For example, some people have been deservedly famous—from beat poet Allen Ginsburg to rock pioneer Fats Domino—without having had much money. It can seem unfair since other artists or merchants adapt their innovations. There are no guarantees that artistic renown leads to resources. But, still, one must be blunt, direct, and self-honest. I have given you my example. *What are you after?* You cannot harness the psyche without concentration.

If the one-word expression eludes you, or if it requires augmentation, use the exercise that appears in the chapter "Mantra Magick." You can combine both approaches: a one-word focus and a mission-oriented affirmation.

Sex Transmutation

This passage involves an exercise that I have described in other writings but that I am presenting for the first time in this book. Sex transmutation is, I believe, if not quite the "missing link" then at least *a critical complementary factor* to enacting your psyche's energies.

In 1948, success writer Napoleon Hill wrote in *Think Your Way to Wealth*:

> The emotion of sex is nature's own source of inspiration through which she gives both men and women the impelling desire to create, build, lead, and direct. Every great artist, every great musician, and every great dramatist gives expression to the emotion of sex transmuted into human endeavor.

The urge toward sexuality, Hill wrote, is the creative impulse of life expressing itself through the individual. He did not limit sexuality to procreation or physical pleasure. He taught, in a manner that squares with New Thought and other spiritual traditions including tantra, that sexuality expresses itself in every area of human creativity. We are driven to function as generative, creative beings in all ways: artistically, commercially, intimately, and in health, communication, athletics, travel, culture, profession, and finance. Whenever you strive to *actualize your visions*—whether as a soldier, student, scholar, or salesman—you are operating from this vital, life-building impulse.

Once you cultivate this awareness you can *transmute* the sexual urge. The method is simple: When you experience sexual arousal, at times of your individual and private choosing, rather than seek some form of physical release, *you purposefully redirect your thoughts and energies along the lines of a cherished project or piece of work*. Through the mental act of redirecting yourself from physical expression to creative expression, you harness and place the sexual urge at the back of whatever you seek to achieve. This, Hill taught, adds vigor, creativity, and intellectual prowess to your efforts. I have personally found this simple, magickal act distinctly powerful. (I write about it further in *Cosmic Habit Force* and *The Power of Sex Transmutation*.)

Let there be no misunderstanding: *this practice does not call for celibacy or denial of desire*. In fact, Hill personally underscored the importance of sex not only as a physical release but also for therapeutic and stress-reducing purposes. The point, rather, is that you are capable of harnessing this innate life force *at specific times and moments of your choosing* to elevate your energies and abilities in a manner beyond what you may think is possible. It involves a simple shift in mental focus. Experiment with this technique.

Acceptance of Channels

As noted, whatever reaches you will most likely arrive through institutions, structures, and groundwork already laid. Hence, on the second day of my practicing this exercise, I received an offer to appear on a television show from a producer with whom I had already gainfully collaborated. The offer did not come from "out of the blue," but was something for which I had ardently prepared and in an area where I had already proven myself and established relationships.

We sometimes reject opportunities because they seem, by polarity, either routine or implausible. But pause carefully. Your deliverance may arise from a source that you are likely to overlook. Religious and ethical history abounds with parables and myths of gods, spirits, or kings who approach someone disguised as a wanderer or stranger. The person who demonstrates hospitality is showered with unforeseen rewards. Honor this prospect.

For example, literally as I am writing this passage, I heard from director Ronni Thomas. Ronni and I had just released a documentary called *The Kybalion*, based on the 1908 occult adaptation of Hermetic principles. On its first day of launch, the surrealistic exploration shot to an unlikely #3 on the iTunes list of top documentaries. Less than a week later, Ronni asked: "Sure it's a total longshot but any way to get the film in front of David Lynch?" I had published David's 2006 book *Catching the Big Fish*. I replied, "Let me think on that. I have his email (or what used to be). It is the one and only favor I may get to ask him. What would I be asking him to do?"

Rather than overthinking it, I reflected back on the lines I had immediately written. Was I prepared to take my own advice and act on an uncertain impulse? I searched for David's email address thinking I had left it on an old computer, which I powered up. But I could not recall the password. The operating system gave me a prompt: "Atkinson lowercase." The password was *kybalion*. (Atkinson is the author behind the occult book's pseudonymous byline, "Three Initiates.") But the email I had did not work, so I sent the film link to a mutual friend asking if he would forward it. He wrote back quickly to say that he would and that he would also follow up. It was more than I had hoped for.

*   *   *

I could at this point continue with lots of related stories and their outcome. I have already argued that linear time is illusory. Hence, something that you or I have done in the so-called future may be impacting our circumstances right now, or what we experience as right now. So, rather than proceed in the cause-and-effect paradigm, let me step out of it. (I will return.)

Does my outcome, or any outcome, serve to "prove" my point about mind causation? You as the reader of this book can venture your own determination as to the ending of this story—or your own story. True happiness, Emerson reasoned, is the "triumph of principles." My principle in this book is that you are a cocreating being, an outlet of ineffable cause, and a participant in interdimensional reality.

The aim of this participation is self-expression. This is why I eschew the idea of transcending desires. It is, of course, possible to give up something, once attained, for something greater. But the taking or retooling of your desires, either by tradition or peer opinion, is an abrogation of self.

I offer a mantra: *I am a being of Infinite Intelligence and I attain my highest self-expression.* We live and die by assumptions—why not this one? If it is truth, which I believe it is, you stand to gain immensely. If it is false, you claim the title of honor: to have tried. In no case is it delusion: delusion is a disastrous distraction and a goad toward ruinous behavior. This is an ideal of vigor.

"Need and struggle," William James wrote in his lecture and essay "Is Life Worth Living?" in 1895, "are what excite and inspire us; our hour of triumph is what brings the void." Hence, we must forever move and search, like the bird-lizard.

I have offered you guiding principles, evidence, and methods. Now, *try*.

*   *   *

What happened in my story? I began this book with the vow to tell you the truth—and I will end it that way.

On the day that I wrote these words, we learned that *The Kybalion* received an award from an Italian film festival. But my mutual friend also got in touch to say that David is hugely busy on a deadline, sends his love, but cannot watch the movie.

Am I dispirited? No. As the day began, I reflected on a principle that I have now noted several times: *the point of life is self-expression*. This includes independence of thought. I also came to another realization. There is, in public life, one thing more important to me than fame, as I have described it. And that is telling the truth.

The road that I have taken, and that I encourage you to embark on, is itself a thought form as much as a terrain. It has its genesis within you. Every bend and turn cannot be determined or foreseen. Its paths are not always smooth or without switchbacks, rocks, and bumps—sometimes severely so, depending on countervailing laws and forces. But the road is exquisitely your own; it shapes you as much as you do it. Your responsibility is to your greatest conception of self. But it must also be realized that everything is a polarity. Let that inform your choices.

I conclude *Daydream Believer* on this note not because it sounds some trumpet of triumph but because it reflects *what you will experience*. You will know victories, defeats (perhaps temporary and purposeful defeats—remember what we considered in "School of War"), and uncertain places from which to continue your search. I conclude this book from an uncertain place. This is not because I had planned to but because it is the truth. It is also the truth that *mind power works*. I venture that within a short time of completing this book you will receive confirmation of that. And when that occurs, you will do what is more important than any conclusion: you will write the next chapter of the unfolding expansion of the human mind.

Appendix

Depression and Metaphysics

This piece originally appeared at Medium *on January 16, 2018. It received a considerable outpouring of response. I include it here because I want to explore additional options around issues of depression or anxiety, which are not always constructively dealt with in the alternative spiritual culture.*

*　　*　　*

Having worked in spiritual publishing for more than 20 years, I have had the mixed blessing of seeing how the sausages get made.

I have personally witnessed bestselling inspirational and metaphysical writers—including some you may avidly read and follow—behave with truculence, anxiety, and occasional freakouts. (In their defense, they have probably seen the same from me.)

I have experienced coworkers running into my office in tears after some author known for dedication to mindfulness, meditation, or "spiritual activism" tore them a new one over a petty or perceived slight or inconvenience.

The fact is that the spiritual search does not equate with or necessarily result in emotional health. Too often, the search can actually serve as a diversion from the workaday issues of accountability, maturity, and maintenance of normative relationships.

To be sure, I have often written in defense of positive-mind metaphysics. I have witnessed motivational philosophies (such as those espoused by Anthony Robbins) and programs of spiritual mutual aid (such as Alcoholics Anonymous) make a great difference in the lives of people in recovery. But when someone is suffering from crippling depression or intense anxiety, the urging to "be positive," in whatever form, can come across like telling a bullied kid to "stand up" to a physically stronger and more intimidating opponent: It may be an ideal, but it is often a psychological, and perhaps physical, impossibility.

As someone who has long written and spoken in favor of the therapeutic benefits of contemporary spirituality, I also believe that real treatment requires a complex of factors: cognitive, meditative, spiritual, and, sometimes, pharmacological. I discourage a knee-jerk reaction against SSRIs or other psychoactive drugs within certain quarters of the New Age or alternative spiritual culture.* I have

---

* As of this writing, I take—and benefit from—an SNRI. SSRIs and SNRIs, among other psychopharmacological drugs, are highly individualized in response. They require research and a constructive relationship with a caregiver. Some object that these drugs are over-prescribed, which is probably

witnessed people combining meds with the practice of Transcendental Meditation, for example, with encouraging results.

Traditional psychology and psychiatry and the self-enacting energies of the mind can form a powerful complement. Indeed, psychiatrists have noted that expectation of recovery from depression is often the key factor in whether any recovery occurs at all. I have personally witnessed psychological and emotional recovery begin when an individual makes a commitment to undergo a serious form of treatment, such as electroshock therapy or hospitalization. In some cases, relief starts to arrive *before* the treatment actually commences. I know of cases where the treatment itself became unnecessary or was more efficacious than expected because improvement was already in process following the patient's commitment and *before* the start date. Therapists have observed that the commitment itself—and the willingness it represents to charge at a problem with all available resources—is therapeutically meaningful. The sense of personal agency that arises when you cross a threshold, when you commit to withholding nothing in pursuit of a solution, can amount to the solution that is sought. The mental act is catalyzing.

Programs of spiritual development and religious traditions can be a great help in this regard. In *The Miracle Club*, I write about the experience of Emily Grossman,

---

true. Depression or anxiety sometimes respond to a combination of exercise, eating habits, meditation, and sleep. I am transparent about my use of a prescription because, in cases where pharmacological treatment is helpful or needed, I want no such option stigmatized.

an extraordinary mental health professional, who began the long road back from a diagnosis of bipolar disorder through her own spiritual search combined with traditional medicine.

At the outset of Emily's road to recovery in the late 1990s, her younger sister Pam, a powerful artist and seeker, handed Emily a copy of Anthony Robbins' self-help book *Awaken the Giant Within*. The book gave Emily a renewed sense of inner drive and pushed her to explore new possibilities in treatment.

A coterie of journalists and social critics regard Robbins, the mountainous life coach and purveyor of a *you-can-do-it* ethos, as something of a joke or huckster. He is no such thing. His message of self-possibility has saved lives. It opened Emily to options.

After bouncing in and out of jobs, Emily began to regain her footing. She moved to New York City in 2005 to attend Teacher's College at Columbia University, from which she graduated the following year. At the time, she half-jokingly told a classmate, "One day, I'm gonna move to California and become a Buddhist." The friend replied, "Well, I'm from California, and I'm a Buddhist, and there's a meeting tonight." That marked her introduction to the daily chanting of *nam myoho renge kyo*, the core practice of Nichiren Buddhism.*

---

* This is a mantra originally written in Sanskrit and reformed into thirteenth-century Japanese. Derived from the title of the classical Buddhist text the Lotus Sutra, the phrase means roughly: "I dedicate myself to the mystic law of cause and effect." Chanting these four sounds—*nam myoho renge kyo*—forms the heart of what is called Nichiren Buddhism, named for its founder, a thirteenth-century Buddhist priest, and practiced today by Soka Gakkai International, or SGI.

"Very soon after I started practicing," Emily said, "I noticed that I was not as symptomatic—I wasn't feeling as depressed. In fact, I was feeling happy. My medicine—which hadn't changed—was working better."

Like me, Emily grew up in a traditional Jewish household; in her case, in Marlboro, New Jersey. I had a small orthodox bar mitzvah at a synagogue in New Hyde Park, Queens. Neither place is on the leading edge of New Age spirituality. But during her recovery, Emily experienced what I consider a breakthrough spiritual insight.

While she was experimenting with the ideas of Robbins, Deepak Chopra, Sharon Salzberg, and other alternative spiritual thinkers, and while at the start of her journey into Buddhism, Emily prayed to the God of her childhood "for a practice that reflected everything I was reading in those books."

Rather than feeling that she was abandoning her childhood tradition, Emily *asked* her old tradition to open a new door for her: "I chanted and I said, 'God, I'm going to be talking to you in a different way now.'" Look at her remark again: "God, I'm going to be talking to you in a different way now." That statement displays great moral aptitude—and summarizes the challenge and courage of New Age and positive-mind metaphysical practice. We are beings of radical ecumenism. Our myriad religious traditions, while using vastly different liturgies and sometimes harboring different aims, nonetheless serve as interlocking chains that can deliver us to what is intimately needed, even if a method or practice lies outside the borders of a tradition itself. The paradox of religion is that it can deliver you to solutions beyond its own premises—including those of traditional psychology and psychiatry.

When coping with emotional duress or mental illness, I endorse taking a "D-Day" approach: Throw everything you have at your problem. See what works. Radically (and maturely) experiment. Rule out nothing. Spirituality is not a panacea or all-in-one treatment for severe depression, anxiety, or any emotional disorder—just as psychology alone cannot substitute for meaning or a search for the greater.

The twentieth-century spiritual teacher Jiddu Krishnamurti observed, "Truth is a pathless land." When confronting personal crisis, never feel bound by any one path, including the spiritual.

Index

About the Author

Ebru Yildiz

Mitch Horowitz is a historian of alternative spirituality and one of today's most literate voices of esoterica, mysticism, and the occult. He is among the few occult writers whose work touches the bases of academic scholarship, national journalism, and subculture cred. Mitch is a writer-in-residence at the New York Public Library, lecturer-in-residence at the Philosophical Research Society in Los Angeles, and a PEN Award-winning historian whose books include *Occult America; One Simple Idea; The Miracle Club*; and *Uncertain Places. The Washington Post* says Mitch "treats esoteric ideas and movements with an even-handed intellectual studiousness that is too often lost in today's raised-voice discussions." He has discussed alternative spirituality across the national media and collaborated

with Emmy-nominated director Ronni Thomas on the feature documentary *The Kybalion*, shot on location in Egypt.
Mitch's books have appeared in Arabic, Chinese, Korean,
Portuguese, Italian, and Spanish. China's government has
censored his work. Visit him at MitchHorowitz.com